The Leadership Spectrum

Barbara Welss Eversole

The Leadership Spectrum

A Continuum of Empathetic Leader Behaviors

Barbara Welss Eversole
Indiana State University
Terre Haute, IN, USA

ISBN 978-3-031-73556-1   ISBN 978-3-031-73557-8   (eBook)
https://doi.org/10.1007/978-3-031-73557-8

This Palgrave Macmillan imprint is published by the registered company Springer Nature Switzerland AG
The registered company address is: Gewerbestrasse 11, 6330 Cham, Switzerland

If disposing of this product, please recycle the paper.

I dedicate this book to my two sons, Birch and Christopher, in the hopes that they may someday become Super Empathetic Compassionate leaders; and to my sister Claudia, the most Super Empathetic Compassionate leader I know.

Acknowledgment

This book would not have been possible without the loving support and encouragement of my beloved spouse and full-time partner for over thirty years, Charles. I cannot thank him enough.

CONTENTS

1   **Introduction**   1
      Conclusion   9
      References   9

Part I   Negative Leaders

2   **The Dark Triad**   17
      Evil, Morality, and Empathy   18
        Evil and Morality   18
        Empathy   18
      Toxic Leadership   20
      The Dark Side of Leadership   21
        The Dark Triad   21
      Gender and the Dark Triad   32
      Culture and the Dark Triad   33
      Conclusion   34
      References   34

3   Bad Leader/Abusive Supervisor/Destructive Leader   47
   Defined   48
   Traits   48
   Behaviors   49
   Prevalence   49
   Outcomes   50
   Gender and Abusive Supervision/Destructive Leadership   50
   Culture and Abusive Supervision/Destructive Leadership   51
   Conclusion   52
   References   52

4   Ineffective, Bullying Leaders   57
   Defined   58
   Traits   58
   Behaviors   58
   Prevalence   59
   Outcomes   60
   Gender and Ineffective Leadership and Workplace Bullying   60
   Culture and Ineffective Leadership and Workplace Bullying   61
   Conclusion   61
   References   62

5   Uncivil Leaders   67
   Defined   68
   Behavior   68
   Prevalence   69
   Outcomes   70
   Gender and Incivility   71
   Culture and Incivility   71
   Conclusion   72
   References   72

Part II   Positive Leaders

6   Civil Transactional Leader   79
   Civility   79
   Defined   80
   Behaviors   80
   Outcomes   80
   Transactional Leadership   83

	Defined	83
	Behaviors	83
	Outcomes	84
	Gender and Civil Transactional Leaders	84
	Culture and Civil Transactional Leaders	84
	Conclusion	85
	References	85
7	**Effective, Caring Leaders**	93
	Effective Leader Behaviors	94
	Managerial Caring	96
	Gender and Effective, Caring Leaders	98
	Culture and Effective, Caring Leaders	99
	Conclusion	100
	References	101
8	**Coaching Mindset Transformational Leader**	105
	Coaching	105
	Defined	106
	Traits	106
	Behaviors	108
	Prevalence	109
	Outcomes	109
	Transformational Leadership	109
	Defined	109
	Behaviors	110
	Outcomes	110
	Gender and Coaching Transformational Leaders	111
	Culture and Coaching Transformational Leaders	112
	Conclusion	113
	References	113
9	**Super Empathetic Compassionate Servant Leaders**	121
	Servant Leaders	122
	Traits	123
	Behaviors	123

Outcomes   123
Compassionate Leaders   124
Authentic Leaders   125
Resonant Leaders   126
Adaptive Leaders   126
Related Descriptions   127
Exemplars of Super Empathetic Leaders   128
Gender and Super Empathetic Leaders   130
Culture and Super Empathetic Leaders   131
Conclusion   131
References   132

Part III   From Negative to Positive

10   Leadership Development—How to Progress from a Negative Leader to a Positive One (Or Make a Positive Leader Even Better!)   141
Uncivil to Civil   142
Civil to Super Empathetic   144
   Training in Compassionate Leadership   145
Leader Derailment   145
   Why Do We Have Bad Leaders   146
Effectiveness of Leadership Development   153
Developing Dark Triad/Bad Leaders   154
   Character Development   154
   Coaching Interventions   154
   Training and Development Interventions   155
   Treatment for Zero Degrees of Empathy   155
Conclusion   156
References   157

Epilogue   167

Index   169

CHAPTER 1

Introduction

Abstract This introduction introduces the reader to the problem of the poor relationship between bosses and their subordinates. While employees leave bosses rather than organizations, the turnover cost of destructive and abusive supervision is enormous. Yet most leadership books research good leaders rather than bad ones. This leadership book looks at leaders along a spectrum of behaviors from bad leaders to great leaders, with uncivil leaders in the middle. Unlike other leadership books, empathy of the leader is the distinguishing variable. The introduction describes the structure of the book.

Keywords Bosses · Turnover · Leadership · Empathy

A popular song by Alan Jackson and Jimmy Buffet about it being 5:00 somewhere hits a chord in the national consciousness. Thank goodness it's five o-clock somewhere, because the boss is making us crazy. Research shows that people don't leave jobs, they don't leave organizations, they leave bad bosses (Goleman et al., 2002; Hogan, 2017; Tate & White, 2005). This book is about bosses. Leaders, managers, and supervisors are all bosses. They have many functions in organizations, but most also serve as direct supervisors to subordinates, no matter what level they are in an organization. Even the CEO has direct subordinates that they supervise;

in fact, often this is one of the most difficult parts of their job, more difficult than steering the company, than mission or vision, than dealing with competitors, than managing the budget, than any of the high-level tasks of the senior manager (Perlman, 2024). Dealing with direct reports is also the task of the frontline supervisor, who needs to help find what motivates the employees of the company. There are 21–38 million bosses, and over 90% of employees in the U.S. work for a boss (Sutton, 2012). If retention of good people is key to an organization's success, and if turnover is costly to an organization, then it is critical for an organization to focus on how leaders at all levels of the organization either effectively or ineffectively manage their followers.

Despite the ubiquitousness and importance of this task in organizations, there is ample evidence that this is not done effectively in most organizations. Turnover is high (41% in 2023, Award.co, 2024) and engagement is low (68% disengaged, Gallup, 2023). Kerns (2021) notes that at some point, all of us will have worked or will work for a bad leader. "Regardless of their formal titles, ineffective, incompetent and abusive leaders account for a great deal of workforce stress, low performance and diminished well-being" (Kerns, 2021, p. 219). A leader's behavior has substantial impact on his or her people and their significant others. Robertson and Barling (2014) found a relationship between well-being of employees and their leader's behavior. As Sutton (2012) noted "…bosses pack a wallop, especially on their direct reports. Bosses shape how people spend their days and whether they experience joy or despair, perform well or badly, or are healthy or sick. Unfortunately, there are hordes of mediocre and downright rotten bosses out there, and big gaps between the best and the worst" (p. 20).

About a third of CEOs are forced out of their positions (Whitehead, 2021). According to the Institute of Crisis Management's 2023 annual report, executive dismissals have increased from 2019 to 2022 from 2.19% to 5.8% (ICM, 2023). Sachs (2019) notes that CEOs are focused on the short term, with 78% of them responding that they have only 90 days in which to prove themselves.

Abbasi and Hollman (2000) estimated that the cost of turnover to U.S. companies is around $1 million for every ten managerial employees who leave their positions, or about $11 billion every year. For technical employees, the costs can be 100 to 150% of salary; for C-suite turnover, over 200% (Heinz & Whitfield, 2024).

Around 79% of employees who leave say that they left because they were not appreciated (Sturt & Nordstrom, 2018). Hogan (2019) noted in a recent interview that almost 70% of employees would be willing to take a pay cut if their immediate supervisor would be terminated; similarly, 65% of workers would rather fire their supervisors than get a raise (Casserly, 2012). 58% say they trust strangers more than their boss (Sturt & Nordstrom, 2018). The least pleasant and most stressful component of an employee's position is their direct supervisor (Harms et al., 2017). Rath and Harter (2010) of the Gallup organization found that employees do not enjoy being around their supervisors, preferring to do chores instead of being with them. 65% of employees surveyed reported that working with their immediate supervisor was the worst part of their jobs (Hogan, 1994). In a study of an international hotel chain, Basch and Fisher (2000) found that nine out of ten times interactions between employees and their bosses led to negative emotions—such as disappointment, hurt feelings, anger, frustration, disgust, and sadness.

Citing a 2016 Gallup poll, only 18% of managers were reported as being good at leading their people (Hougaard, 2018). Abusive supervisors are common, and they are damaging their employees (Pfeffer, 2018; Schyns & Schilling, 2013). Erickson et al. (2007) found in their study of U.S. and Australian employees that one-third of them rated their supervisors as bad leaders, exhibiting behaviors such publicly scolding them in front of others, whispering about them, stealing their ideas, and playing favorites.

In an extreme example of destructive leadership and its impact on employees, in 2010 Foxconn, a Taiwanese company that manufactures i-Phones for Apple in China, made headlines when eighteen employees attempted suicide (fourteen succeeding), because of harsh treatment by their managers (Merchant, 2017). This treatment included humiliation, unfair fines, and broken promises. One employee stated, "If the boss finds any problems, they don't scold you then. They scold you later, in front of everyone, at a meeting" (Merchant, 2017).

In Gallup's, 2023 *State of the Global Workplace Report*, they stated clearly that leaders need to change the way people in organizations are managed. Low engagement could cost up to $8.8 trillion. Gallup found that hating your job is even worse than not having one. With about 60% of employees quietly quitting, and 18% actively disengaged, the best thing that organizations can do is "give them a better manager" (Gallup, 2023, p. 1). Training managers to be coaches raised engagement from 8 to

18%. Estimates range from 13 to 36% of workers work with dysfunctional leaders (Rose et al., 2015). Blank (2021) notes that supervisors using influence based on compliance and coercion is common in today's organizations, becoming "worst bosses": bullying, manipulating, and forcing subordinates to submit to their demands. Employees being abused by supervisors affects their families too (Hoobler & Brass, 2006).

By most measures, this relationship between supervisor and supervisee is not going well. However, most of the literature about leadership, management, and supervision focuses on successful leaders, managers, and supervisors (Schyns & Schilling, 2013). Less literature focuses on the ineffective, or even dangerous, among them or "bad" dysfunctional leaders (Erickson et al., 2007; Rose et al., 2015), although some scholars have begun to note both the increasing incidence and the costs of bad leadership (Aasland et al., 2010; Kaiser et al., 2015; Kilfedder & Litchfield, 2014; McCleskey, 2013; Schulte et al., 2015). And even fewer books and articles focus on the leaders and managers who are in between, the ones who arguably can still be transformed or developed into better supervisors, who could make a tremendous difference in the lives of their direct reports, who could reduce turnover, increase retention, increase engagement, increase productivity, and thereby increase the profitability of their organizations.

The spectrum aims to take a different approach. By looking at supervisory characteristics and behaviors, and the character of the supervisor themselves, along a continuum of behaviors and characteristics of supervisors, my book offers fresh insights into the relationship between the supervisor and their direct reports. Almost every leader is also a boss. Like Patel et al. (2022), I follow Yukl (1989) and do not distinguish between leaders and managers; I mean leadership to mean supervisory leadership (House & Aditya, 1997) not strategic leadership.

"Leadership exists within a relationship" (Spain, 2019, p. xv). Wood et al. (2021) noted the importance of the leaders' relationships in organizations:

> Relationally, the leadership process includes *how* the group is actually conducted in accomplishing the goal--the means employed--to move from point A to point B, that is, either in a moral, humanistic, conscious, and emotionally intelligent manner (e.g. Goleman & Boyatzis, 2017), or in a mostly immoral, instrumental, unconscious, or emotionally oblivious way. (p. 54)

Using a spectrum, one can see how a managerial leader can be developed from an uncivil supervisor to an effective one; a leader who needs to evolve their character before being able to be a better supervisor can be recognized; and one can recognize where on the spectrum a particular leader would fit. Ultimately, the book serves as a model of leadership characterization and development useful to academic scholars, to scholar-practitioners who coach and consult in leadership development, and to managers in organizations themselves.

A word about gender and global culture is appropriate here. It is unclear how much of an effect they may have on the leadership spectrum and on leadership effectiveness. A meta-analysis done in 2005 showed that 80% of the time, men and women differed very little in terms of IQ, attitudes, job performance, and motivation (Hyde, 2014). Research that measures leadership effectiveness shows that men and women do not differ (Powell, 2014). However, if emotional intelligence (EI) and empathy are keys to better relationships between leaders and their direct reports, and women tend to be more emotionally intelligent and/or utilize EI in authentic, transformational leadership styles, women may be more likely to be more effective leaders (Chamorro-Premizic, 2019; Eagly et al., 2003; Gartzia & van Engen, 2012; Joseph & Newman, 2010; Powell, 2014). Significantly, women outscore men on average on Baron-Cohen's (2011) empathy quotient, as well as reading a person's feelings merely from their eyes. One of the most significant gender differences found is in preference: women prefer to work with people, while men prefer to work with things (Su et al., 2009). In any case, fewer women reach the senior management level of organizations than men do (Castle-Rogers, 2022). Fewer than 10% of firms from 27 countries are led by women CEOs (Heidrick & Struggles, 2024). In the U.S., only 8.8% of the Fortune 500 companies' CEOs are women, and only 30% of their board of directors (Catalyst, 2018). The numbers are about the same in the U.K. for the FTSE 100 corporations, 7% and 29% respectively (Vinnicombe et al., 2018).

As far as national culture is concerned, Hamlin et al. (2012) have shown that when it comes to supervisory relationships, global culture may not have a moderating effect. It may not make much difference what part of the world that the behavior exists, effective and ineffective leadership behavior is the same. There may be nuances due to national culture; for example, every subordinate wants to be treated with respect by their leader, however, what is respectful behavior may vary by culture

(Porath & Gerbasi, 2015). The influence of gender and culture on the leadership spectrum will be further explored in the coming chapters.

Why another leadership book? Leadership as a construct is still not well understood. Northouse in his definitive text on leadership, concluded: "After decades of dissonance, leadership scholars agree on one thing: They can't come up with a common definition for leadership" (2021, p. 5). Northouse does, however, offer his own helpful working definition: "*Leadership* is a process whereby an individual influences a group of individuals to achieve a common goal" (Northouse, 2021, p. 6). I argue that leadership is a process of *individual* influence, whether it be their *behavior* or their *personality traits* that drive that behavior. As Leo McCann, Professor of Management at the University of York has noted, "Despite the millions of words written and spoken about leadership, still we see chronic problems with the ways in which organizations, firms, and nations are led" (Amazon.com, n.d.). There is a problem with bad leaders, such as corporate psychopaths. According to Boddy et al. (2021), "Corporate psychopaths look and sound successful to those above them, appear to be "star" managers and employees who are worthy of further promotion. Arguably, the result of all this is the crisis of leadership and sustainability that the world is now facing" (p. 80). Moreover, having a psychopathic supervisor actually predicts an employees' intention to leave due to lower levels of job satisfaction (Babiak & Hare, 2019). According to Erickson et al. (2007) in order to really understand leadership, we need to study both good and bad leadership; otherwise, we would be like doctors ignoring disease in favor of focusing on health. There is a lack of scholarship on bad leadership (Kellerman, 2005; Krasikova et al., 2013).

Why this leadership book? This book has been thoroughly researched from secondary sources from the best academics and scholar-practitioners in the management, human resource and organization development, and industrial/organizational psychology fields and augmented with primary research data collected by the author and colleagues. The book's unique approach of looking at leadership personality, behavior, and outcomes through the lens of a spectrum will be useful to both scholars and practitioners in understanding a critical management issue.

The notion of the spectrum, with empathy as a distinguishing variable, is my book's contribution to leadership development studies. The supervisor or leader who has little, or no empathy is at one end of the spectrum, while the supervisor or leader with super empathy, either by nature or with skill, is at the other. There are a multitude of books on leadership, all kinds of leadership; however, the notion of a spectrum as a range of behaviors of leaders as supervisors, with the relationship between the supervisor and supervisee as the focus, using empathy as the distinguishing characteristic of the leader, is unique.

As Babiak and Hare (2019) put it, "We believe that many bosses are good people, well trained and positively motivated; others simply are "bad bosses"; and still others are corporate psychopaths" (p. 229). Leaders, no matter what else they do, in organizations as CEOs, managers, or frontline managers are also supervisors. They do many other things in organizations and can be highly effective in other areas. But if they are abusive to their direct reports, eventually, they will fail. Even if they make their sales, great profits, they do remarkable things, they will fail. The idea of my book is to give managers the tools to intervene before this happens. That's the heart of my book and its contribution: supervisory leadership can be conceptualized as a spectrum of behaviors with zero empathy and poor leadership on one end and high empathy and effective leadership on the other. Empathy has been found to be one of the traits that a manager/supervisor needs to have in order to influence their employees' intent to leave (as well as their job satisfaction and organizational commitment) (Mathieu et al., 2015). As Baron-Cohen (2011) put it, "empathy itself is the most valuable resource in our world" (p. 153).

Recently, scholars have found that bad leadership is an important area of research, noting that psychopaths are often found in the higher levels of organizations (Pavlić & Međedović, 2019); they may even be more prevalent there than in the general population (Boddy, 2015)—in fact, as much as three times as much (Babiak et al., 2010). These psychopathic leaders are not good for organizations (Shank et al., 2018; van Scotter & Roglio, 2020) or their employees (Valentine et al., 2018). According to Boddy et al. (2021), "the topic of leader psychopathy has been re-emphasized as an important area of study in management" (p. 72). Schyns et al. (2022) agreed, noting that interest in psychopaths in the workplace has increased recently.

Boak (2021) noted that although currently leaders are expected to be more consultative and less directive, and workers have more rights globally than ever before, destructive leaders still abuse power and damage those who work for them. Kerns (2021) noted, "There are too many bad leaders causing adverse impacts on people in organizations" (p. 220). And Babiak and Hare (2019) add, "Retention of talented employees is the key to organizational success and we now know that at least one factor influences employee retention, and that is the direct supervisor's core personality" (p. 226). According to Burke (2006) "A consideration of the dark side of leadership is likely to increase our ability to effectively develop the leaders organizations will need in the twenty-first centuries" (p. 98).

Another central notion of my book is that something can be done about "bad" leaders. As also argued by Örtenblad (2021), my book operates under the notions that there are "bad" leaders, that there are enough of them that it is problematic, that the situation can be improved upon, and that we need to understand why we have "bad" leaders in the first place.

The structure of my book is ordered around a spectrum of bad leaders to good leaders, ending with how to make bad leaders better. The first four chapters describe the negative types of leader/supervisors, starting from the worst type of leader, the dark triad leader with zero degrees of empathy. The next four chapters describe behaviors of increasingly effective leader/supervisors, ending with the leader with the greatest amount of empathy. It is important to note that empathy is necessary but not sufficient for great leadership. There are many other necessary elements that go into being a great leader/supervisor. The main thesis for my book is that empathy is one of them.

Every one of us lies on a spectrum of empathy from low to high which generates a distribution. This distribution has been measured as a normal distribution by Baron-Cohen (2011) which he calls the empathy bell curve. Zero degrees of empathy lies at one end of the curve with Level 6 at the other end (super empathy). I conceptualize the leadership spectrum in the same way, with the dark triad leaders and Empathetic leaders at either end of a normal curve. The idea is that at either end of the spectrum, leadership behaviors occur less frequently than normal. The notion is that Super Empathetic leaders are as rare in the population of leaders as the dark triad leaders, with the vast majority of leaders being uncivil to civil, creating a leadership spectrum. My argument is that the leadership spectrum's eight descriptions of leaders maps approximately to Baron-Cohen's (2011) seven levels of empathy. These descriptions lie on a continuum, so don't have distinct borders. Importantly, the chapters help readers place themselves or their leader on the spectrum.

Finally, the last chapter discusses how to develop ineffective leaders into effective ones. The worst leaders, the dark triad leaders with no empathy, require the most intervention and may not be able to be transformed into better leaders. Empathy is a skill that can be learned (Gerdes et al., 2011); however, not everyone is capable of learning or willing to learn this skill. In Chapter 2, we will learn about the neurobiology of the dark triad, and the difficulty of changing the basic nature of these leaders. Character development is always a possibility; however, it is difficult and not always achievable. Leaders are both born and made; however, not every leader can be developed.

CONCLUSION

Leaders can be described on a spectrum of traits and behaviors based on the amount of empathy that they have, with the dark triad leaders on one end and super empathetic leaders on the other, with uncivil and civil leaders in the middle of the spectrum. Ultimately, this is a hopeful book about leadership development; that leaders can be identified along the spectrum, and that steps can be taken to help develop leaders where they are into better leaders, leaders who will no longer abuse their direct reports, but will help them become the best employee that they can be and lead better lives.

REFERENCES

Aasland, M. S., Skogstad, A., Notelaers, G., Nielsen, M. B., & Einarsen, S. (2010). The prevalence of destructive leadership behavior. *British Journal of Management, 21*(2), 438–452.

Abbasi, S., & Hollman, K. (2000). Turnover: The real bottom line. *Public Personnel Management, 29*, 333–342.

Amazon.com. *Book review.* https://www.amazon.com/Reflexive-Leadership-Management-Practice-Essentials/dp/0367511169/ref=sr_1_1?crid=2VW W2Q3DUGNWM&dib=eyJ2IjoiMSJ9.ygt0KhPiTCaJXHmqQOZQQcbD b7HsinYrDaaN0RDJVZrGjHj071QN20LucGBJIEps.HT4HekRd2vL4YwW dOuMh5kXzy2oisFDJ9n9-LEqJuyY&dib_tag=se&keywords=Reflexive+leader ship+in+context&qid=1721407925&s=books&sprefix=reflexive+leadership+ in+context%2Cstripbooks%2C105&sr=1-1. Accessed 19 July 2024.

Award.co. (2024, June 7). *Understanding employee turnover rates (and how to improve them).* https://www.award.co/blog/employee-turnover-rates. Accessed 28 July 2024.

Babiak, P., & Hare, R. D. (2019). *Snakes in suits* (2nd ed.). Harper Business.

Babiak, P., Neumann, C. S., & Hare, R. D. (2010). Corporate psychopathy: Talking the walk. *Behavioral Sciences & the Law, 28*(2), 174–193.

Baron-Cohen, S. (2011). *The science of evil: On empathy and the origins of cruelty.* Basic Books.

Basch, J., & Fisher, C. D. (2000). Affective events-emotion matrix: A classification of job-related events and emotions experienced in the workplace. In N. Ashkanasy, W. Zerbe, & C. Hartel (Eds.), *Emotions in the workplace: Research, theory and practice* (pp. 36–48). Quorum Books.

Boddy, C. R. (2015). Organizational psychopaths: A ten-year update. *Management Decision, 53*(10), 2407–2432.

Boak, G. (2021). Shining a light on toxic leadership. In A. Örtenblad (Ed.), *Debating bad leadership: Reasons and remedies* (pp. 105–120). Palgrave Macmillan.

Boddy, C., Boulter, L., & Fishwick, S. (2021). How so many toxic employees ascend to leadership. In A. Örtenblad (Ed.), *Debating bad leadership: Reasons and remedies* (pp. 69–86). Palgrave Macmillan.

Blank, W. (2021). What explains the quality of today's leaders? In A. Örtenblad (Ed.), *Debating bad leadership: Reasons and remedies* (pp. 166–181). Palgrave Macmillan.

Burke, R. J. (2006). Why leaders fail: Exploring the dark side. *International Journal of Manpower, 27*(1), 91–100. https://doi.org/10.1108/014377206 10652862

Casserly, M. (2012, October 17). Majority of Americans would rather fire their boss than get a raise. *Forbes.* https://www.forbes.com/sites/meghancasserly/2012/10/17/majority-of-americans-would-rather-fire-their-boss-than-get-a-raise/?sh=30c94f6c6610. Accessed 26 May 2024.

Castle-Rogers, A. (2022). Social capital implications for the gender gap in organizational leadership through a lens of intersectionality. In K. Yeager, D. S. Chai, & L. Xei (Eds.), *2022 Academy of Human Resource Development Virtual Conference, April 19–21, 2022.*

Catalyst. (2018). *Women CEOs of the S&P 500.* https://www.catalyst.org/research/women-in-the-workforce-united-states/. Accessed 16 July 2024.

Chamorro-Premizic, T. (2019). *Why do so many incompetent men become leaders? (And how to fix it).* HBR Press.

Eagly, A. H., Johannesen-Schmidt, M. C., & van Engen, M. L. (2003). Transformational, transactional, and lassiz-faire leadership styles: A meta-analysis comparing women and men. *Psychological Bulletin, 129*(4), 569–591.

Erickson, A., Shaw, J. B., & Agabe, Z. (2007). An empirical investigation of the antecedents, behaviors, and outcomes of bad leadership. *Journal of Leadership Studies, 1*(3), 26–43.

Gallup. (2023). *State of the global workforce 2023 report.* https://www.gallup.com/workplace/349484/state-of-the-global-workplace.aspx. Accessed 18 February 2024.

Gartzia, L., & Van Engen, M. (2012). Are (male) leaders "feminine" enough? Gendered traits of identity as mediators of sex differences in leadership styles. *Gender in Management: An International Journal, 27*(5), 296–314. https://doi.org/10.1108/17542411211252624

Gerdes, K. E., Segal, E. A., Jackson, K. F., & Mullins, J. L. (2011). Teaching empathy: A framework rooted in social cognitive neuroscience and social justice. *Journal of Social Work Education, 47*(1), 109–131.

Goleman, D., & Boyatzis, R. (2017). Emotional intelligence has 12 elements. Which do you need to work on? *Harvard Business Review, 84*(2), 1–5.

Goleman, D., Boyatzis, R., & McKee, A. (2002). *Primal leadership: Realizing the power of emotional intelligence.* HBR Press.

Hamlin, R. G., Patel, T., Ruiz, C., & Whitford, S. (2012). Towards a universal taxonomy of perceived managerial and leadership effectiveness: A multiple cross-case/cross-nation study of effective and ineffective managerial behaviour. In *Proceedings of the 13th UFHRD International Conference of Human Resource Development Research and Practice across Europe.* UFHRD.

Harms, P. D., Credé, M., Tynan, M., Leon, M., & Jeung, W. (2017). Leadership and stress: A meta-analytic review. *The Leadership Quarterly, 28*(1), 178–194.

Heidrick & Struggles (2024). *Where are the women CEOs?* https://www.heidrick.com/-/media/heidrickcom/publications-and-reports/where-are-the-women-ceos.pdf. Accessed 18 February 2024.

Heinz, K., & Whitfield, B. (2024, July 17). *The true costs of employee turnover.* https://builtin.com/recruiting/cost-of-turnover. Accessed 28 July 2024.

Hogan, R. (1994). Trouble at the top: Causes and consequences of managerial incompetence. *Consulting Psychology Journal: Practice and Research, 46*(1), 9.

Hogan, R. (2017). *Personality and the fate of organizations.* Psychology Press.

Hogan, R. (2019). *Robert Hogan on Management TV: True leadership is not a matter of politicking or charisma.* Interview. Youtube https://www.yoube.com/watch?v=nfsemaE0TLo. Accessed 29 January 2024.

Hoobler, J. M., & Brass, D. J. (2006). Abusive supervision and family undermining as displaced aggression. *Journal of Applied Psychology, 91*(5), 1125–1133.

Hougaard, R. (2018, September 9). The real crisis in leadership. *Forbes.* https://www.forbes.com/sites/rasmushougaard/2018/09/09/the-real-crisis-in-leadership/?sh=473280693ee4. Accessed 22 May 2024.

House, R. J., & Aditya, R. N. (1997). The social scientific study of leadership: Quo vadis? *Journal of Management, 23*(3), 409–473. https://doi.org/10.1177/014920639702300306

Hyde, J. S. (2014). The gender similarities hypothesis. *American Psychologist, 60*(6), 581–592. https://doi.org/10.1037/0003-066X.60.6.581

ICM. (2023). *Institute of crisis management annual report*. ICM. https://crisis consultant.com/wp-content/uploads/2023/07/ICM-Annual-Crisis-Report-for-2022.Issued-July-13.2023-1.pdf. Accessed 17 February 2024.

Joseph, D. L., & Newman, D. A. (2010). Emotional intelligence: An integrative meta-analysis and cascading model. *Journal of Applied Psychology, 95*(1), 54–78. https://doi.org/10.1037/a0017286

Kaiser, R. B., LeBreton, J. M., & Hogan, J. (2015). The dark side of personality and extreme leader behavior. *Applied Psychology, 64*(1), 55–92.

Kellerman, B. (2005). How bad leadership happens. *Leader to Leader, 2005*(35), 41.

Kerns, C. D. (2021). Bad leaders: Some realities, reasons and remedies. In A. Örtenblad (Ed.), *Debating bad leadership: Reasons and remedies* (pp. 219–234). Palgrave Macmillan.

Kilfedder, C., & Litchfield, P. L. (2014). Well-being as a business priority. In C. L. Cooper & F. A. Huppert (Eds.), *Interventions and policies to enhance well-being* (pp. 358–386). Wiley Blackwell.

Krasikova, D. V., Green, S. G., & LeBreton, J. M. (2013). Destructive leadership: A theoretical review, integration, and future research agenda. *Journal of Management, 39*(5), 1308–1338.

Mathieu, C., Fabi, B., Lacoursiere, R., & Raymond, L. (2015). The role of supervisory behavior, job satisfaction and organizational commitment on employee turnover. *Journal of Management & Organization, 22*(1), 1–17. https://doi.org/10.1017/jmo.2015.25

McCleskey, J. (2013). The dark side of leadership: Measurement, assessment, and intervention. *Business Renaissance Quarterly, 8*(2/3), 35–53.

Merchant, B. (2017, June 18). Life and death in Apple's forbidden city. *The Guardian*. https://www.theguardian.com/technology/2017/jun/18/foxconn-life-death-forbidden-city-longhua-suicide-apple-iphone-brian-merchant-one-device-extract. Accessed 21 February 2024.

Northouse, P. G. (2021). *Leadership: Theory and practice* (9th ed.). Sage.

Örtenblad, A. (2021). Background and introduction. In A. Örtenblad (Ed.), *Debating bad leadership: Reasons and remedies* (pp. 3–34). Palgrave Macmillan.

Patel, T., Hamlin, R. G., & Louis, D. (2022). Toward a generic framework of negative manager/leader behavior: A comparative study across nations and private sector industries. *European Management Review*, 1–17. https://doi.org/10.1111/emre.12507

Perlman, E. (2024, June 4). The three hardest and most unexpected challenges of being a CEO. *Forbes*. https://www.forbes.com/sites/forbesbusinesscouncil/2024/06/04/the-three-hardest-and-most-unexpected-challenges-of-being-a-ceo/#:~:text=Managing%20people%20is%20perhaps%20one,and%20culture%20of%20the%20company. Accessed 28 July 2024.

Powell, G. N. (2014). Sex, gender, and leadership. In S. Kumra, R. Simpson, & R. J. Burke (Eds.), *The Oxford handbook of gender in organizations* (pp. 249–268). Oxford University Press.

Pavlić, I., & Međedović, J. (2019). Psychopathy facilitates workplace success. *Psihološka istraživanja, 22*(1), 69–87. https://doi.org/10.5937/PSISTR A22-19287

Pfeffer, J. (2018). *Dying for a paycheck: How modern management harms employee health and company performance.* Harper Business.

Porath, C. L., & Gerbasi, A. (2015). Does civility pay? *Organizational Dynamics, 44*(4), 281–286. https://doi.org/10.1016/j.orgdyn.2015.09.005

Rath, T., & Harter, J. (2010). *Well-being: The five essential elements.* Gallup Press.

Robertson, J., & Barling, J. (2014). Lead well, be well: Leadership behaviors influence employee well-being. In P. Y. Chen & C. L. Cooper (Eds.), *Work and well-being* (pp. 236–251). Wiley Blackwell.

Rose, K., Shuck, B., Twyford, D., & Bergman, M. (2015). Skunked: An integrative review exploring the consequences of the dysfunctional leader and implications for those employees who work for them. *Human Resource Development Review, 14*(1), 64–90.

Sachs, M. (2019, November 13). The CEO disconnect: Balancing short-term wins with long-term growth. *CEO News.* https://www.ceotodaymagazine. com/2019/11/the-ceo-disconnect-balancing-short-term-with-long-term-growth/. Accessed 18 February 2024.

Schulte, P. A., Guerin, R. J., Schill, A. L., Battachararya, A., Cunningham, T. R., Pandalai, S. P., Eggerth, D., & Stephenson, C. M. (2015). Considerations for incorporating "well-being" in public policy for workers and workplaces. *American Journal of Public Health, 105*(8), 31–44.

Schyns, B., & Schilling, J. (2013). How bad are the effects of bad leaders? A meta-analysis of destructive leadership and its outcomes. *The Leadership Quarterly, 24*(1), 138–158.

Schyns, B., Gauglitz, I. K., Wisse, B., & Schütz, A. (2022). How to mitigate destructive leadership: Human resources practices that mitigate dark triad leaders' destructive tendencies. In D. Lusk and T. L. Hayes, (Eds.) *Overcoming Bad Leadership in Organizations.* (pp. 251–274). Oxford University Press. https://doi.org/10.1093/050/9780197552759.003.0013

Shank, C. A., Dupoyet, B., Durand, R., & Patterson, F. M. (2018). *The decision making of a financial psychopath.* https://acfr.aut.ac.nz/__data/ass ets/pdf_file/0006/190608/Decision-Making-of-the-Financial-Psychopath. pdf. Accessed 29 January 2024.

Spain, S. M. (2019). *Leadership, work and the dark side of personality.* Academic Press.

Stone, M. H. (2020). The place of psychopathy along the spectrum of negative personality types. In S. Itzkowitz & E. F. Howell (Eds.), *Psychoanalysts, psychologists and psychiatrists discuss psychopathy and human evil* (pp. 82–105). Routledge.

Sturt, D., & Nordstrom, T. (2018, March 8). *10 shocking workplace stats you need to know*. https://www.forbes.com/sites/davidsturt/2018/03/08/10-shocking-workplace-stats-you-need-to-know/?sh=4c608976f3af. Accessed 22 May 2024.

Su, R., Rounds, J., & Armstrong, P. I. (2009). Men and things, women and people: A meta-analysis of sex differences in interests. *Psychological Bulletin, 135*(6), 859–884. https://doi.org/10.1037/a0017364

Sutton, R. I. (2012). *Good boss, bad boss: How to be the best... and learn from the worst*. Business Plus.

Tate, R., & White, J. (2005). *People leave managers... not organizations! Action-based leadership*. iUniverse.

Valentine, S., Fleischman, G., & Godkin, L. (2018). Villains, victims, and verisimilitudes: An exploratory study of unethical corporate values, bullying experiences, psychopathy, and selling professionals' ethical reasoning. *Journal of Business Ethics, 148*, 135–154.

Van Scotter, J. R., & Roglio, K. D. D. (2020). CEO bright and dark personality: Effects on ethical misconduct. *Journal of Business Ethics, 164*, 451–475.

Vinnicombe, S., Doldor, E., & Sealy, R. (2018). *Female FTSE Board Report 2018: Busy going nowhere with the executive pipeline*. Cranfield University.

Whitehead, J. (2021). Is 'bad leadership" a problem worth addressing? In A. Örtenblad (Ed.), *Debating bad leadership: Reasons and remedies* (pp. 35–46). Palgrave Macmillan.

Wood, J. D., Meister, A., & Liu, H. (2021). Defining the good, the bad, and the evil. In A. Örtenblad (Ed.), *Debating bad leadership: Reasons and remedies* (pp. 47–65). Palgrave Macmillan.

Yukl, G. (1989). Managerial leadership: A review of theory and research. *Journal of Management, 15*, 254–289.

PART I

Negative Leaders

CHAPTER 2

The Dark Triad

Abstract This chapter describes the worst bad leader, ones from the dark triad, with zero degrees of empathy. The dark triad consists of corporate psychopaths, malignant narcissists, and Machiavellians. These toxic dark side leaders cause considerable damage to their subordinates because they lack empathy with them. The chapter describes what empathy is along with the behavior and characteristics of these leaders and the outcomes for their subordinates and organizations.

Keywords Dark Triad · Corporate Psychopaths · Narcissists · Machiavellians · Empathy

The leader on this end of the spectrum can be described as lacking empathy—one might even say they are evil, if we define evil as lacking in empathy (Baron-Cohen, 2011). With no ability to understand how their behavior affects others, they are free to be abusive toward their direct reports. Psychologists would also label these folks as dark triad or dark leaders. For Wood et al. (2021), dark leaders are leaders who have privilege, control and power because they lead in an immoral and evil way; yet evil is built into leadership (Wood & Liu, 2012). Therefore, a discussion of dark leadership necessarily means a discussion of evil, morality, and empathy.

© The Author(s), under exclusive license to Springer Nature   17
Switzerland AG 2025
B. W. Eversole, *The Leadership Spectrum*,
https://doi.org/10.1007/978-3-031-73557-8_2

Evil, Morality, and Empathy

The question of evil is a highly personal one for leaders, as it relates to one's self-awareness of their wholeness, their ability to be good or bad, and to be able to know this without deceiving themselves (Jung, 1989). The concept of evil, however, can also be thought of as the absence of empathy (Baron-Cohen, 2011), rather than the absence of morality, when thinking of evil leaders.

Evil and Morality

For Baron-Cohen (2011), any discussion of evil belongs not in relation to religion, but in biology and social sciences. To say that psychopaths are merely evil does not give us any explanatory power (Baron-Cohen, 2011). The dictionary defines evil as "morally reprehensible" or "arising from actual or imputed bad character or conduct" and "causing harm" (Merriam-Webster, 2014). Book et al. (2015b) has suggested that the core behavioral traits of the dark triad can serve as a definition of evil itself. This, however, also does not help us in our quest to understand evil and morality. Decety (2013) noted that the callous disregard that psychopaths have for others contributes to amoral behavior. Luckily, as Mendez (2009) put it, "Humans have an innate moral sense" (p. 16). Goleman (2006) notes that humans have social emotions such as shame, embarrassment, remorse and guilt that serve as a moral compass—something that the dark triad lack.

A fuller discussion of evil is beyond the scope of this book; however, the reader is referred to Itzkowitz (2020) and Itzkowitz and Howell (2020). For our purposes, we will adopt Baron-Cohen's (2011) conceptualization of evil as the absence of empathy.

We will now turn to a discussion of the central construct of the book, empathy. We will discuss it in further detail in later chapters as we describe leaders with ever greater levels empathy. We will also discuss emotional intelligence.

Empathy

Empathy comes from the German "Einfühlung," which means, "feeling into" (Lipps, as cited in Gallese, 2001). Baron-Cohen (2011) defines empathy as "Empathy occurs when we suspend our single-minded focus of attention and instead adopt a double-minded focus of attention. Empathy is our ability to identify what someone else is thinking or feeling and to respond to their thoughts and feelings with an appropriate emotion" (pp. 15–16). When we are empathetic, we experience another's feelings (Goleman, 2006). From a neuroscience standpoint, our mirror neuron systems are active, which causes us to move from feeling to action (Goleman, 2006). Empathy has three parts: recognizing the emotions of another; feeling that emotion; and then acting in response to the emotion in a compassionate way (Goleman, 2006). Whether empathy includes action in a compassionate way, or whether compassion is action + empathy (Hougaard & Carter, 2022) may be a matter of scholarly debate; however, for our purposes, empathy is the precursor for action to occur. We will return to a discussion of empathy and compassion when we discuss compassionate leaders at the end of the leadership spectrum.

Social awareness is one of the domains of emotional intelligence (EI) (Goleman & Boyatzis, 2017). The other three are self-awareness, self-management, and relationship management. Social awareness includes primal empathy, attunement, empathic accuracy, and social cognition (Goleman, 2006). Primal empathy is what the German definition is, feeling with others. Attunement means being attuned to others, and empathic accuracy is the understanding (or cognition) of others' feelings. Social cognition is understanding how the social world functions. Acting on one's empathetic feelings would be part of a social facility in Goleman's model of social intelligence, which is as important as emotional intelligence. In Goleman's model, concern is empathy in action, what Baron-Cohen (2011) and Hougaard and Carter (2022) call compassion.

Changes in empathy can be measured in the brain (Preston & de Waal, 2002). "Mirroring occurs whenever our perception of someone automatically activates an image or a felt sense in our own brain for what they are doing and expressing" (Goleman, 2006, p. 59).

Empathy (recognition and response) can be measured using the Empathy Quotient (EQ), a self-report instrument, which produces an empathy bell curve (Baron-Cohen & Wheelwright, 2004), referred to in the Introduction. (EQ can also be used to refer to Emotional Intelligence Quotient; we will use EI instead.) According to Baron-Cohen (2011), every one of us lies on a spectrum of empathy from low to high on the empathy curve. When we commit an evil act, we can think of it as unempathic, whether it is physical or verbal, such as mockery, deception, or abuse. When we commit this evil act, our empathy circuit, or

EQ, temporarily goes down, or off, if we are on the normal part of the empathy curve.

However, if we are on the extreme low end of the empathy curve, or zero degrees negative, then our empathy system is permanently off or down, and then we are like one of the dark triad personalities. We can therefore think of evil as empathy erosion, and those who are evil are at the extreme low end of the empathy curve (Baron-Cohen, 2011; cf. Book et al., 2015b; Heym et al., 2021).

Empathy can also be thought of as a construct that includes affective empathy, cognitive empathy, empathic concern, and empathic distress (Jonason et al. 2013). We will discuss these facets later on; however, the distinction between affective and cognitive empathy is important to understand now. Affective empathy is the kind of empathy that we have been discussing, where emotions are shared, along with mirror neurons and bodily states. Cognitive empathy is a recognition or understanding of another's emotion (or theory of mind) without the emotion. For a complete review and discussion of empathy, affective and cognitive, and theory of mind, see Schurz et al. (2021). Cognitive empathy is important when we discuss the dark triad.

Baron-Cohen (2011) refers to empathy as "the universal solvent. Any problem immersed in empathy becomes soluble" (p. 186). And it's free. Gerdes et al. (2011) agrees: "Lack of empathy underlies the worst things humans can do to one another; high empathy underlies the best" (p. 109). For more reading on empathy, Baron-Cohen suggests *The Empathic Civilization* by Rifkin (2009) and *The Age of Empathy* by de Waal (2009). In Denmark, school-age children are taught empathy, which may contribute to Denmark's status as one of the happiest countries in the world (Addeco group, 2020).

Shoemaker (2012) claimed that "the default position of humans from birth, when it is not interfered with by abuse or illness, is to be empathetic, social, and concerned about their fellow human beings" (p. 817). It seems then, that dark triad leaders are made, rather than born (cf. Hoyk & Hersey, 2008).

Toxic Leadership

Although the term "toxic leadership" was first used by Lipman-Blumen (2005), she was not the first to use the term toxic to describe dysfunctional leadership. Reed (1994) first used the term "toxic executive" to describe abusive leaders. Reed (1994) identified the worst of these toxic leaders as Super Toxic. "They are conflictual, deceitful, they put others down, they steal ideas and take all the credit from others, they interrupt everyone in meetings, they are loners who never participate, they never mentor anyone else, they abuse power, and they are unilateral decision-makers" (p. 259). From a Maslow (1970) point of view, these leaders never had their needs for safety and belonging met. The Super Toxic leader who lacks empathy does extensive damage in organizations.

THE DARK SIDE OF LEADERSHIP

Moshagen et al. (2018) proposed a construct that they called D: the Dark Factor of Personality, or the dark core of personality. D includes not only the dark triad personalities, but also other negative traits such as spitefulness, entitlement, self-interest, egoism, and moral disengagement. They define D as "the general tendency to maximize one's individual utility— disregarding, accepting, or malevolently provoking disutility for others— accompanied by beliefs that serve as justifications; in sum, the utility-based aspects of D specify that individuals high in D, in seeking [their] own utility, pursue behaviors that may negatively affect others and avoid behaviors that unilaterally benefit others, especially if this might incur personal costs" (pp. 657–658). According to Leslie (2022), "Identifying additional personality traits that can damage leadership performance continues" (p 145).

The Dark Triad

These Super Toxic leaders have since been characterized as being "dark" or part of the "dark triad" or the "dark tetrad" with malevolent personality constructs (Boddy et al., 2021; Paulhus, 2014; Visser & Doyle, 2022). The dark triad (psychopathy, narcissism, and Machiavellianism) all share traits such as deceitfulness, manipulation, callousness, and lack of empathy (Jones & Figueredo, 2013). The dark triad personalities exhibit toxic and counterproductive behaviors in the workplace (O'Boyle et al., 2012) as well as enjoying the suffering of their coworkers (James et al., 2014). The dark tetrad adds sadism which should also affect employee well-being in a negative way (Babiak & Hare, 2019; Visser & Doyle, 2022). See Visser and Doyle (2022) for a discussion of sadism as the fourth member of the Dark Tetrad.

The dark triad personality traits that are present in the workplace are subclinical, as they do not impact the functioning of the leader enough for a clinical diagnosis of psychopathy or narcissism (Kaiser et al., 2015). Therefore, leaders can be high to low on these traits (Fatfouta, 2019). *Leaders with high scores on all dark triad traits lack empathy* and are callous toward the welfare of others (Paulhus, 2014). Dark triad leaders are unable to collaborate with others and therefore are unable to work in a team; this often leads to derailment in the organization (Babiak & Hare, 2019). They are unable to share credit, resources, or power (Babiak & Hare, 2019). The three dark triad traits have in common that they have the "tendency to maximize one's individual utility disregarding, accepting, or malevolently provoking disutility for others accompanied by beliefs that serve as justifications" (Moshagen et al., 2018, p. 1). The three dark triad traits leading to the dark triad personalities (psychopaths, narcissists, and Machiavellians) are, however, quite distinct from one another (O'Boyle et al., 2012; Schyns et al., 2022).

The dark triad traits have repeatedly been found to cause organization malfunctioning (LeBreton et al., 2018; Spain et al., 2014). These dark triad traits are negatively correlated with empathy, compassion, and agreeableness (Furnham et al., 2013), yet employees who possess them are more likely to be leaders (Furnham, 2016). In fact, dark triad personalities seek out leadership positions and are more prevalent in them than in the general population because they desire the power, social standing, dominance, and money that they bring (Babiak & Hare, 2019; Grijalva et al., 2015; Jones & Figueredo, 2013). Ultimately, as Stern (2021) correctly notes, "Their psychological traits make them good at fooling people, but ultimately, it is their toxic behavior, not their traits, that destroys their leadership" (p. 155).

At one end of the spectrum, the worst of the worst, the darkest of the dark triad, is the corporate psychopath (Boddy, 2021; LeBreton et al., 2018). Babiak and Hare (2019) noted that psychopaths are the most destructive, dishonest, and treacherous of the dark triad.

Corporate, Successful, Subclinical Psychopaths

"We must be quite clear that we cannot protect everyone. In 2007 I will have these job cuts one way or another. By the window or by the door." France Telecom's CEO Didier.

France Telecom (now Orange) made the news when during a restructuring process in the 2000's, senior management started a campaign of "moral harassment" to force state employees with guaranteed life-time employment to leave the organization (Schofield, 2019). As a result of this bullying campaign, the families of nineteen employees who committed suicide, along with twenty other employees affected by managerial abuse, were part of a prosecution case against three senior managers, including the CEO (Schofield, 2019). His comments to his senior managers about the restructuring of the organization led to his conviction of responsibility for the eighteen suicides at France Telecom (France Telecom...2019). Rarely is a corporate psychopath brought to account in such a public way. The case was seen a landmark one for workers and their managers in France. It is notable that one of the siblings of one of the victims remarked about the senior managers who were convicted, "They never had any remorse during the trial; they constantly put the blame on subordinates."

McCullough (2022) shared stories collected from members of the Chief Financial Officers (CFO) Leadership Council of CEOs who they believed could have been psychopaths. Some included:

- "CEO made employees wait outside his office, often for hours, to talk to him about routine matters. Even the CFO was made to wait outside his office in a classic power trip.
- Autocratic CEO fired a well-respected engineer "just to make a statement." He fired anyone who challenged him, explaining there was no reason to second-guess him because he was always right and needed people to execute his vision rather than challenge it.
- CEO requests reports but does not read them. Routinely tells employees they are stupid and untalented. Encourages the CFO to yell at employees to inspire fear
- CEO would show up to work and begin yelling at an employee (usually someone in sales) for no obvious reason. He believed in managing through intimidation and considered yelling at people a motivational tool."

In fact, Cheang and Appelbaum (2015b) noted that corporate psychopathic behavior includes "glibness, manipulativeness, extreme dishonesty and grandiosity... lack of empathy, lack of emotion and affect, lack of remorse, and a failure to accept responsibility" (p. 167). Didier Lombard was a classic corporate psychopath, until he was convicted.

Successful corporate psychopaths "have been referred to as successful psychopaths due to their ability to avoid confrontation with legal authorities" (Cheang & Appelbaum, 2015a, p. 167). Didier Lombard was unable to avoid the legal ramifications of his behaviors; and his conviction was upheld three years later (Orange exec's guilty..., 2022).

Defined. This leader is known as a subclinical or successful psychopath, rather than a clinical, criminal psychopath (Boddy, 2021). They are successful psychopaths because they do not get into trouble with the law (Cheang & Appelbaum, 2015a). A psychopathic leader is defined as one who is ruthless and has no "conscience, regret, care, responsibility, empathy, compassion or truthfulness" (Boddy, 2017, p. 70). Subclinical psychopaths are attracted to the money, prestige, and power of senior leadership (Chiaburu et al., 2013), while they alienate and severely bully employees (Boddy et al., 2021; Kaiser & Hogan, 2007). Psychopathy is a combination of personality traits and behaviors formed by the interaction of genetics and social and environmental factors (Babiak & Hare, 2019).

Traits. Cleckley (as cited in Baron-Cohen, 2011) in his book, *The Mask of Sanity*, did pioneering research on psychopaths, and listed these characteristics of a psychopath:

- superficial charm
- lack of anxiety or guilt
- undependability and dishonesty
- egocentricity
- inability to form lasting intimate relationships
- failure to learn from punishment
- poverty of emotions
- lack of insight into the impact of their behavior
- failure to plan ahead (p. 68)

Psychopaths have a hard time perceiving sadness or fear in the voices or faces of others (Goleman, 2006). Baron-Cohen (2011) noted that although psychopathy is a personality disorder, the important thing is that they have zero degrees of empathy; they have an underactive empathy circuit, which results in their ability to be cruel. Their cruelty is in a cold and calculated way, completely detached from the emotions of others, they have a need to dominate (Baron-Cohen, 2011). Goleman (2006) agrees: "Empathy is the prime inhibitor of human cruelty: withholding our natural inclination to feel with another allows us to treat another as an It" (p. 117).

Psychopaths are impulsive as well as antisocial along with low anxiety and empathy (Mullins-Sweatt et al., 2010; Schyns et al., 2022). They are totally preoccupied with themselves, willing to do whatever it takes to get what they want, and violently react when they don't (Baron-Cohen, 2011). They are egocentric and lacking in loyalty to anyone (Babiak & Hare, 2019).

Since psychopaths are such accomplished liars, it is difficult to diagnose them using self-report measures (Baron-Cohen, 2011). Psychopaths have less arousal when looking at distressed people in photos, implying less empathy (Blair, 1999). Psychopaths also have difficulty in recognizing fear in people's facial expressions, while feeling no fear themselves (Dutton, 2016). It is this inability to experience fear that is responsible for their inability to experience affective empathy (Blair, 2017), thereby allowing the psychopath to harm and manipulate others (Hare & Neumann, 2008). Moreover, psychopaths do not show the expected brain activity when shown emotional words (Lorenz & Newman, 2002).

Psychopaths do not feel guilty if they hurt someone; rather they use others as a means to an end and discard them once they have fulfilled their purpose (Babiak & Hare, 2019). They are insincere, unreliable, and do not understand themselves or their impact on others (Babiak & Hare, 2019). Suffering from affective dysfunction (Seara-Cardoso et al., 2012) and having no affective empathy, they do have cognitive empathy, or theory of mind, meaning they can recognize others' emotions (Blair et al., 2018; Decety et al., 2013; Drayton et al., 2018). This allows the psychopath to manipulate and exploit others, since they have a cognitive understanding of their emotions without being able to empathize with them (Book et al., 2015a; Patrick, 2018).

Behaviors. Psychopaths are willing to lie about their accomplishments, their qualifications, and take the credit for work they did not do (Babiak & Hare, 2019). Lacking any modesty at all, they appear self-confident and strong to their own superiors (Babiak & Hare, 2019). When they fail or make mistakes, they never hold themselves accountable but blame others (Babiak & Hare, 2019). It is impossible to predict what they will do, and they often overreact to perceived slights or disrespect, causing coworkers and direct reports to walk on eggshells (Babiak & Hare, 2019). Corporate psychopaths are more likely to degrade or ridicule their direct reports, be forceful and aggressive (Jones & Neria,

2015; Mathieu et al., 2014) and bully them (Gudmundsson & Southey, 2011).

Emotions have little importance or interest to corporate psychopaths, and they do not care what happens to their employees. Psychopaths, however, appear quite charming and can fake their emotions easily (Porter et al., 2011). They promise what they cannot deliver; they mislead and persuade followers who need leaders who appear determined, strong, and authoritative (Boddy et al., 2021). Moreover, according to Babiak and Hare (2019) psychopaths are also doomed to repeat their dysfunctional behaviors because they are unable to learn from their experiences.

Prevalence. A psychopath has a diagnosis of antisocial personality disorder (DSM-5, 2013). Three percent of men in the general population (1% of women) have this personality disorder (Baron-Cohen, 2011). A subset of people with this disorder has psychopathic personality disorder—only about 1% of the general population (Babiak & Hare, 2019; Chamorro-Premuzic, 2019).

There may be as many as 3–4 times the rate of pyschopaths on corporate boards than in the general population (Boddy, 2015; Chamorro-Premuzic, 2015); in fact, there may be more psychopaths as top executives than in the entire population (Ronson, 2012). A study in 2016 estimated that 21% of executives were psychopaths (Brooks, 2016). "Nonetheless, based on many anecdotal reports and on our own observations, it is likely that psychopathic individuals make up much more than 1 percent of business managers and executives" (Babiak & Hare, 2019, p. 176). Babiak and Hare (2019) estimate 10% of the general population fall in a "gray zone," having some psychopathic traits but are not psychopaths. Self-serving with a tendency to lie and manipulate, without self-doubt or fear, they are charming and disguise their lack of affect (Barelds et al., 2018).

Outcomes. This super-toxic psychopathic leader (Lipman-Blumen, 2005; Reed, 1994) causes serious and continuous damage to the employees and teams that they lead. O'Boyle et al. (2012) found a relationship with job performance and counterproductive work behaviors (CWB). Corporate pyschopaths are able to create what Boddy et al. (2021) call "a culture of fear" in organizations. Subordinates managed by these dark leaders are not able to intellectually or emotionally respond appropriately, therefore the leader keeps their power (Webster et al., 2016). Moreover, whether or not an employee was a psychopath was found to be the best predictor of harassment in the workplace (Mathieu &

Babiak, 2016b). Psychopaths use intimidation, coercion, and bullying, which hurts people and disrupts work (Babiak & Hare, 2019). Psychopathic leaders have been shown to have ill effects on the well-being and career success of direct reports (Volmer et al., 2016), using abusive tactics (Boddy, 2015).

According to Sanecka (2013) subordinates who worked for supervisors who were subclinical psychopaths had less job satisfaction, less satisfaction with their supervisor, and less organizational commitment. Leaders with psychopathic traits also caused employees to have psychological distress (Babiak et al., 2010).

Unfortunately, corporate psychopaths are good at looking like high-potential leaders, and even inferior performance reviews and complaints from subordinates do not change their superiors' opinions (Babiak et al., 2010). Instead of leading effectively or focusing on being competent at work, psychopathic leaders promote themselves and network, managing upwards to get noticed and promoted more frequently than would be expected given their prevalence in organizations (Babiak et al., 2010; Boddy et al., 2021). They rise quickly and easily through the organization (Babiak et al., 2010), charming their own leaders while intimidating their subordinates and manipulating others (Jonason et al., 2012; Lilienfeld et al., 2014; Mathieu et al., 2013) which looks like persuasion and an ability to influence others (Babiak et al., 2010). Without any interest in emotional relationships, their focus on work is mistaken for commitment (Boddy et al., 2021). Add the lack of a conscience to their lack of emotional connection, the corporate psychopath can easily make tough decisions, remaining calm under pressure, and being rational (Babiak & Hare, 2019). Their charm looks like self-confidence and charisma (Babiak et al., 2010). Yet psychopathic supervisors score low on measures of transformational and transactional leadership, and high on laissez-faire (Mathieu & Babiak, 2015; Westerlaken & Woods, 2013). Their focus on immediate gratification and short-term goals makes it difficult for them to plan for the long term (Jones & Paulhus, 2014). Babiak and Hare (2019) remarked, "Notably, psychopathic leaders are not likely to be successful leaders either" (p. 228).

The next member of the dark triad is the Narcissist.

Narcissists
Narcissus was an ancient Greek hunter in mythology known by all for his beauty, who fell in love with his own reflection in a pool of water.

Defined. Like psychopathy, narcissism is a personality disorder (Babiak & Hare, 2019). According to the DSM-5, someone with narcissistic personality disorder has a need for admiration, along with a pattern of grandiosity, a lack of empathy, and feelings of entitlement and superiority (Babiak & Hare, 2019). Narcissists also have zero degrees of empathy (Baron-Cohen, 2011).

Traits. According to scholars who study them, narcissists are callous, tend toward being exploitative, need excessive amounts of attention, and feel superior (LeBreton et al., 2018; Paulhus & Williams, 2002; Wright et al., 2013). Narcissists have a drive for glory and power and are self-confident (Jakobwitz & Egan, 2006). Having no humility, they are self-centered and boastful and therefore easily offend others (Baron-Cohen, 2011). Pincus et al. (2009) referred to "narcissistic grandiosity" as "interpersonally exploitive acts, lack of empathy, intense envy, aggression, and exhibitionism" (p. 367). According to Sedikides and Campbell (2017), narcissism is a

> self-absorbed, self-aggrandizing, vanity-prone, arrogant, dominant, and manipulative interpersonal orientation. Narcissists are preoccupied with their own sense of specialness and importance, and with fantasies of power, beauty, and acclaim. They manifest low levels of empathy, shame, or guilt, while boasting about their ability, thinking of themselves as exceptional or unique, demanding adulation, lashing out at rivals, and not shying away from interpersonal, business, or political brawls. (p. 400)

According to Baron-Cohen (2011), narcissists have zero degrees of empathy, just like psychopaths. Jonason and Krause (2013) also found that narcissism was associated with limited ability to identify feelings and low affective empathy, yet they have cognitive empathy (Pajevic et al., 2018). Recent studies (George & Short, 2018; Jankowiak-Siuda & Zajkowski, 2013) show a neural empathy deficit in narcissists. Moreover, narcissism is negatively associated with perspective-taking and emotional intelligence as well as empathy (Vonk et al., 2013).

Leaders who have a prominent level of narcissism exhibit "arrogance, self-absorption, entitlement, fragile self-esteem, and hostility" (Rosenthal & Pittinsky, 2006, p. 671). They exhibit "an unusually high level of self-love, believing that they are uniquely special and entitled to praise and admiration" (Judge et al., 2009). Despite their feelings of grandiosity, they are actually insecure and feel inferior (Jones & Paulhus, 2014; Kets de Vries, 2014). Pride is their tragic flaw (Spain, 2019).

Narcissism is measured using the NPI (Raskin & Hall, 1979; Rotolo & Bracken, 2022), which is a self-report measure with 40 pairs to choose from, such as "I like to be the center of attention," paired with "I prefer to blend in with the crowd" (Rotolo & Bracken, 2022).

Nevertheless, narcissistic leaders are very charismatic and visionary (Maccoby, 2000) and confident (Kets de Vries, 2014); yet lacking in moral sensibility (Blair et al., 2008). Narcissistic leadership, as a style of leadership, is one where the leader's need for power and admiration outweighs their care and concern for others or the institution that they lead (Homer & Fredericks, 2005; Rosenthal & Pittinsky, 2006).

Malignant Narcissists. When narcissists' lack of empathy and sense of entitlement become aggressive, antisocial, and destructive, they become malignant narcissists (Babiak & Hare, 2019; Germain, 2018). Malignant narcissists are sadists who enjoy the suffering of others and are paranoid (Germain, 2018).

Behavior. Narcissists don't have any choices in their behavior, so they admire themselves rather than paying any attention to anyone else (Babiak & Hare, 2019). Others are used as objects and exploited by the narcissist (Baron-Cohen, 2011). Feelings of insecurity and inferiority can lead narcissists to being hypersensitive to criticism (Rosenthal & Pittinsky, 2006). Narcissists generally lack any care for other people, while they have an excessive sense of their own self-worth and importance (Vonk et al., 2013). They feel that they deserve special treatment from others because they are special (O'Boyle et al., 2012). They feel like they can be rude to everyone else (Linton & Power, 2013). Narcissistic leaders are autocratic, abuse power, have bursts of anger, claim privilege, and do not acknowledge others (Cote, 2018). They are abusive toward others (Germain, 2023) as well as being antagonistic toward others (Leckelt et al., 2015) thinking others are inferior to them (Rosenthal & Pittinsky, 2006). Schyns et al. (2022) surmised that narcissistic leaders only behave in an aggressive manner when their ego is threatened, e.g., when they receive negative feedback from a direct report. Without any empathy, they do not have any regrets and do not care about the feelings or needs of their subordinates (Goleman, 2006). When narcissistic leaders are not threatened, they are less likely to become aggressive toward subordinates (Jones & Neria, 2015; Jones & Paulhus, 2010).

Prevalence. Only about 1% of the population have narcissistic personality disorder (Babiak & Hare, 2019; Baron-Cohen, 2011).

Outcomes. Narcissistic leaders are likely to try to dominate, control, and demean their direct reports (Tokarev et al., 2017); if unsuccessful they may become angry leading to counterproductive behaviors in the workplace (Penney & Spector, 2002). Arrogance has been found to negatively predict task performance (Johnson et al., 2010). While narcissism is associated with the emergence of leaders, it is not associated with effectiveness (Grijalva et al., 2015) and their ratings decrease over time (Ong et al., 2016). Braun (2017) reviewed studies of narcissistic leaders and found two studies where narcissists negatively impacted their followers in terms of their emotions, organizational citizenship behaviors (OCB), and (CWB) (Braun et al., 2018; Martin et al., 2016). The lack of empathy exhibited by narcissistic leaders during a crisis is especially harmful (Simmons, 2020). Narcissists' lack of empathy may lead to their lower leadership ratings over time (Rosenthal & Pittinsky, 2006). See Braun (2017) for an excellent discussion of narcissist leaders.

Next on the spectrum and in the dark triad are the Machiavellians.

Machiavellian Leaders

The notion of Machiavellian leaders in organizations was first conceived of by Christie and Geiss in 1970, so called after the sixteenth century Italian author, Niccolo Machiavelli, of *The Prince*, a treatise on getting and using political power.

Defined. Machiavellian leaders have some of the same characteristics as psychopaths; however, they are not as ruthless. Like other dark triad leaders, they lack empathy, but they also are calculating and instrumental when in relationships with others (Jones & Paulhus, 2014). Machiavellians would definitely qualify to have zero degrees of empathy, although Baron-Cohen (2011) did not include them in his book as they are not considered a personality disorder in the DSM-5 (Furnham, 2022). Christie and Geiss (1970) defined Machiavellianism as "a strategy of social conduct that involves manipulating others for personal gain" (p. 285). It is more like a belief or philosophy as opposed to a personality disorder, one that is marked by lack of emotion and self-interested, cynical, manipulative behavior (Furnham, 2022). Beller and Bosse's (2017) research suggested that Machiavellianism is more a dimension than a category.

Traits. Machiavellians dislike people and have a practical and cynical view of morality, using flattery, lying, and their lack of affect and empathy to manipulate others to get what they want (Christie & Geiss, 1970; Schyns et al., 2022); they are expedient rather than principled (O'Boyle et al., 2012). They believe that others are gullible and stupid (Spain, 2019). However, Szabó and Bereczkei (2017) found that there was a positive relationship between Machiavellianism and the perspective-taking part of cognitive empathy. Other scholars (Wai & Tiliopoulos, 2012; cf. Pajevic et al, 2018) have also found that Machiavellians possess cognitive empathy, helping them deceive and manipulate others (Smith, 2006). They are not necessarily good at manipulating others, however (Spain, 2019).

Machiavellians are tested using the MACH-IV instrument (Rotolo & Bracken, 2022) which was developed by Christie and Geiss (1970). It is a self-report instrument with 20 items and a 5-point scale. One of the items, for example, includes, "It is hard to get ahead without cutting corners here and there."

Behaviors. Machiavellianism is a way of getting opportunities and personally benefiting by being unethical (Jakobwitz & Egan, 2006). Spurk et al. (2016) found that Machiavellianism is positively correlated with being able to earn a leadership position. Machiavellian leaders are primarily interested in getting more power and don't mind being unethical and dishonest as long as it benefits them personally (Judge et al., 2009). Strategies include deception and manipulation, with a focus on self-interest (Leslie, 2022). These strategies of focusing on their own goals at the expense of others are completed by engaging in immoral behaviors such as exploitation along with low affect (Christie & Geiss, 1970; Dahling et al., 2009; LeBreton et al., 2018; Paulhus & Williams, 2002; Spain et al., 2014). Machiavellians use strategic action as their manipulation is goal-oriented (Schyns et al., 2019) and power-seeking (Rauthmann & Kolar, 2012). Vernon et al. (2008) argued that Machiavellians are influenced by and adjust to their environment. They are cunning as well as deceptive and manipulative to get what they want (Esperger & Bereczkei, 2012). They "employ aggressive, exploiting, and devious behavior to achieve personal and organizational goals" (Ricks & Fraedrich, 1999, pp. 197–198), happy to exploit and violate the rights of others (Winter et al., 2004).

As leaders they choose their own self-interest over that of others' (Sakalaki et al., 2007), pursuing their own goals using others as a means to an end (Burris et al., 2013; Schyns et al., 2019). Machiavellian leaders are likely to be abusive (Dahling et al., 2009), bullies (Pilch & Turska, 2015) and hostile (Jones & Neria, 2015).

Prevalence. According to Beller and Bosse (2017), we do not know the prevalence of Machiavellianism.

Outcomes. Machiavellianism has been shown to have ill effects on the well-being and career success of direct reports (Volmer et al., 2016) and is negatively related to OCB (Becker & O'Hair, 2007). Moreover, Machiavellians have low levels of loyalty and commitment to the organization (Thibault & Kelloway, 2020) along with feeling that the organization has not lived up to its obligations to them (Li et al., 2020). They are more likely to have difficulties working with others, leading to problems with work performance (O'Boyle et al., 2012). Viewing the office as a political arena, they maximize their own self-interest rather than that of the organization (Riaz et al., 2019).

Gender and the Dark Triad

Men and women differ in empathy in the brain (Baron-Cohen, 2011). When reading emotions on facial expressions, women have more activity in the empathy circuit than men do (Baron-Cohen et al., 2006). Girls and women also score higher on the EQ than men in the general population (Baron-Cohen & Wheelwright, 2004; Goldenfeld et al., 2005; Wakabayashi et al., 2006). Psychopaths who are men have been researched more often than those who are women (Babiak & Hare, 2019), and more men than women test as psychopaths in the general population (Lynam et al., 2010; Neumann & Hare, 2008). In the workplace, men also score higher than women on self-report instruments (Mathieu & Babiak, 2016a), and as supervisors (Babiak & Hare, 2019). Men are more likely to be Machiavellians than women (Jones & Paulhus, 2009) and more likely to be narcissists than women (Grijalva et al., 2015).

Men, as opposed to women, are more likely to exhibit dark triad traits (Chamorro-Premuzic, 2019; Muris et al., 2017). Jonason et al (2020) studied the dark triad traits globally and found that women in developed countries were less likely to be narcissistic than women in less developed countries. These results were similar to Luo et al. (2023) who found that men scored higher than women on dark triad traits in the U.K., Greece, and China, with the magnitude of the difference being higher in the U.K. Aluja et al. (2022) studied 18 different cultures and found that women scored lower on all three dark triad traits than men in most of the cultures studied. The differences between the genders were greatest in European cultures. Rogoza et al. (2021) similarly found that men scored higher than women on dark triad traits in their study of eight different world regions.

CULTURE AND THE DARK TRIAD

Most studies on the dark triad have taken place in Western contexts (Jonason et al., 2020). Aluja et al (2022) studied 18 cultures and found that somewhere between 6 and 16% of the variance in dark triad traits could be explained by national culture. Jonason et al. (2020) studied the dark triad traits in 49 countries and found that narcissism was more common in less developed countries, a result also found by Rogoza et al. (2021). The impact of national culture on psychopathology has had mixed results (Canino et al., 2010).

Moreover, Arseneault and Catano's (2019) research has questioned the utility of the dark triad framework in Asian cultures. Ma et al. (2021) compared a Chinese (collectivist culture) sample with a U.S. (individualist culture) sample on dark triad traits and work outcomes such as organizational citizenship behavior (OCB), counterproductive work behavior (CWB), and turnover intention. Their findings varied by dark triad type and work outcomes. For psychopathy, they found the same relationship in the U.S. and China—negative correlations with positive work outcomes, and positive correlations with negative work outcomes. For narcissism, findings were mixed. For Machiavellianism, the correlations were different in the U.S. and China; in China, the correlations between Machiavellianism and positive work outcomes were more positive than in the U.S., while the correlations between Machiavellianism and negative work outcomes were more negative in China than the U.S. Another study by Robertson et al. (2016) which studied the dark triad traits in the U.S. and the Philippines found no differences in Machiavellianism related to power distance but found that both narcissism and psychopathy had different relationships to independence and interdependence due to power distance in each country. For example, psychopathy was positively related to interdependence in the Filipino sample, while it was negatively related in the American sample. This all points to a more nuanced understanding of the dark triad in Asian and Southeast Asian cultures.

Ramos-Vera et al. (2023) studied the dark triad personality traits in non-Western countries such as Poland, Brazil, Nigeria, Colombia, and

Peru using structural equation modeling (SEM) and network analysis. Machiavellianism was found to be more relevant in the four countries as opposed to Nigeria. The authors noted that this could have been due to the more collectivist nature of the Latin American countries, where they are more likely to try and avoid political and social changes. Narcissism was present in all five countries.

CONCLUSION

Dark triad leaders—corporate psychopaths, narcissists, and Machiavellians—cause poor outcomes for subordinates and organizations due to their lack of empathy and self-interested behaviors. Now that we have looked at the worst leaders, the dark triad leaders without any empathy, let's turn to the next leaders on the spectrum, abusive and destructive leaders.

REFERENCES

Addeco Group. (2020, August 31). *Empathy? In Denmark they are learning it in school*. https://www.adeccogroup.com/future-of-work/latest-insights/empathy-in-denmark. Accessed 17 July 2024.

Aluja, A., Garcia, L. F., Rossier, J., Ostendorf, F., Glicksohn, J., Oumar, B., Bellaj, T., Ruch, W., Wang, W., Suranyi, Z., Ścigała, D., Čekrlija, Ð., Stivers, A. W., Blas, L. D., Valdivia, M., Jemaa, S. B., Atitsogbe, K. A., Hansenne, M., & Hansenne, M. (2022). Dark triad traits, social position, and personality: A cross-cultural study. *Journal of Cross-Cultural Psychology*, 53(3–4), 380–402.

Arseneault, R., & Catano, V. (2019). An extension of the dark triad and five-factor model to three Asian societies. *Asian Journal of Social Psychology*, 22(4), 358–368.

Babiak, P., & Hare, R. D. (2019). *Snakes in suits* (2nd ed.). Harper Business.

Babiak, P., Neumann, C. S., & Hare, R. D. (2010). Corporate psychopathy: Talking the walk. *Behavioral Sciences & the Law*, 28(2), 174–193.

Barelds, D. P., Wisse, B., Sanders, S., & Laurijssen, L. M. (2018). No regard for those who need it: The moderating role of follower self-esteem in the relationship between leader psychopathy and leader self-serving behavior. *Frontiers in Psychology*, 9, 1281.

Baron-Cohen, S. (2011). *The science of evil: On empathy and the origins of cruelty*. Basic Books.

Baron-Cohen, S., Ring, H., Chitnis, X., Wheelwright, S., Gregory, L., Williams, S., Brammer, M., & Bullmore, E. (2006). FMRI of parents of children with Asperger Syndrome: A pilot study. *Brain Cognition, 61*(1), 122–130.

Baron-Cohen, S., & Wheelwright, S. (2004). The Empathy Quotient (EQ): An investigation of adults with Asperger Syndrome or high-functioning autism, and normal sex differences. *Journal of Autism and Developmental Disorders, 34*(2), 163–175. https://doi.org/10.1023/B:JADD.0000022607.19833.00

Becker, J. A., & Dan O'Hair, H. (2007). Machiavellians' motives in organizational citizenship behavior. *Journal of Applied Communication Research, 35*(3), 246–267. https://doi.org/10.1080/00909880701434232

Beller, J., & Bosse, S. (2017). Machiavellianism has a dimensional latent structure: Results from taxometric analyses. *Personality and Individual Differences, 113*, 57–62. https://doi.org/10.1016/j.paid.2017.03.014

Blair, R. J. R. (1999). Responsiveness to distress cues in the child with psychopathic tendencies. *Personality and Individual Differences, 27*(1), 135–145.

Blair, R. J. R. (2008). Fine cuts of empathy and the amygdala: Dissociable deficits in psychopathy and autism. *Quarterly Journal of Experimental Psychology, 61*(1), 157–170.

Blair, R. J. R. (2017). Emotion-based learning systems and the development of morality. *Cognition, 167*, 38–45. https://doi.org/10.1016/j.cognition.2017.03.013

Blair, R. J. R., Meffert, H., Hwang, S., & White, S. F. (2018). Psychopathy and brain function: Insights from neuroimaging research. In C. J. Patrick (Ed.), *Handbook of psychopathy* (2nd ed., pp. 401–421). Guilford Press.

Boddy, C. R. (2015). Organisational psychopaths: A ten-year update. *Management Decision, 53*(10), 2407–2432.

Boddy, C. R. (2017). Psychopathic leadership a case study of a corporate psychopath CEO. *Journal of Business Ethics, 145*(1), 141–156.

Boddy, C., Boulter, L. & Fishwick, S. (2021). How so many toxic employees ascend to leadership. In A. Örtenblad (Ed.) *Debating Bad Leadership: Reasons and Remedies*. (pp. 69–85). Palgrave Macmillan.

Boddy, C., Boulter, L., & Fishwick, S. (2021). How so many toxic employees ascend to leadership. In A. Örtenblad (Ed.), *Debating bad leadership: Reasons and remedies* (pp. 69–85). Palgrave Macmillan.

Book, A., Methot, T., Gauthier, N., Hosker-Field, A., Forth, A., Quinsey, V., & Molnar, D. (2015a). The mask of Sanity revisited: Psychopathic traits and affective mimicry. *Evolutionary Psychological Science, 1*(2), 91–102. https://doi.org/10.1007/s40806-Ol5-0012.x

Book, A., Visser, B. A., Anthony, A., & Volk, A. A. (2015b). Unpacking "evil": Claiming the core of the dark triad. *Personality and Individual Differences, 73*, 29–38. https://doi.org/10.1016/j.paid.2014.09.016

Braun, S. (2017). Leader narcissism and outcomes in organizations: A review at multiple levels of analysis and implications for future research. *Frontiers in Psychology, 8*(773), 260159. https://doi.org/10.3389/fpsyg.2017.00773

Braun, S., Aydin, N., Frey, D., & Peus, C. (2018). Leader narcissism predicts malicious envy and supervisor-targeted counterproductive work behavior: Evidence from field and experimental research. *Journal of Business Ethics, 151*, 725–741. https://doi.org/10.1007/s10551-016-3224-5

Brooks, N. (2016). *Understanding the manifestation of psychopathic personality characteristics across populations* (Doctoral dissertation, Bond University).

Burris, C. T., Rempel, J. K., Munteanu, A. R., & Therrien, P. A. (2013). More, more, more: The dark side of self-expansion motivation. *Personality and Social Psychology Bulletin, 39*(5), 578–595. https://doi.org/10.1177/014616721 3479134

Canino, G., Polanczyk, G., Bauermeister, J. J., Rohde, L. A., & Frick, P. J. (2010). Does the prevalence of CD and ODD vary across cultures? *Social Psychiatry and Psychiatric Epidemiology, 45*, 695–704. https://doi.org/10. 1007/s00127-010-0242-y

Chamorro-Premuzic, T. (2015). Why bad guys win at work. *Harvard Business Review.* https://hbr.org/2015/11/why-bad-guys-win-at-work. Accessed 10 February 2024.

Chamorro-Premuzic, T. (2019). *Why do so many incompetent men become leaders (and how to fix it).* Harvard University Press.

Cheang, H. S., & Appelbaum, S. H. (2015a). Corporate psychopathy: Deviant workplace behaviour and toxic leaders–part one. *Industrial and Commercial Training, 47*(4), 165–173.

Cheang, H. S., & Appelbaum, S. H. (2015b). Corporate psychopathy: Deviant workplace behaviour and toxic leaders (part two). *Industrial and Commercial Training, 47*(5), 236–243.

Chiaburu, D. S., Muñoz, G. J., & Gardner, R. G. (2013). How to spot a careerist early on: Psychopathy and exchange ideology as predictors of careerism. *Journal of Business Ethics, 118*, 473–486.

Christie, R., & Geiss, F. L. (1970). *Studies in Machiavellianism.* Academic Press.

Cote, R. (2018). Dark side leaders: Are their intentions benign or toxic? *Journal of Leadership, Accountability & Ethics, 15*(2), 42–65. https://doi.org/10. 33423/lae.v15i2.643

Dahling, J. J., Whitaker, B. G., & Levy, P. E. (2009). The development and validation of a new Machiavellianism scale. *Journal of Management, 35*(2), 219–257.

Decety, J. (2013). The neuroevolution of empathy and caring for others: Why it matters for morality. In *New frontiers in social neuroscience* (pp. 127–151). Springer International Publishing.

Decety, J., Chen, C., Harenski, C., & Kiehl, K.A. (2013). An fMRI study of affective perspective taking in individuals with psychopathy: Imagining another in pain does not evoke empathy. *Frontiers in Human Neuroscience, 7*, 489. https://doi.org/10.3389/fnhum.2013.00489

de Waal, F. (2009). *The age of empathy: Nature's lessons for a kinder society.* Crown.

Diagnostic and statistical manual of mental disorders (5th Edition) (DSM-5). (2013). American Psychiatric Association.

Drayton, L. A., Santos, L. R., & Baskin-Sommers, A. (2018). Psychopaths fail to automatically take the perspective of others. *Proceedings of the National Academy of Sciences of the United States, 115*(13), 3302–3307. https://doi.org/10.1073/pnas.1721903115

Dutton, K. (2016). Would you vote for a psychopath? *Scientific American Mind, 27*(5), 50–55.

Esperger, Z., & Bereczkei, T. (2012). Machiavellianism and spontaneous mentalization: One step ahead of others. *European Journal of Personality, 26*(6), 580–587. https://doi.org/10.1002/per.859

Fatfouta, R. (2019). Facets of narcissism and leadership: A tale of Dr. Jekyll and Mr. Hyde? *Human Resource Management Review, 29*(4), 100669.

Furnham, A. (2016). *The elephant in the boardroom: The causes of leadership derailment.* Springer.

Furnham, A. (2022). Bright and dark side of personality: The relationship between personality traits and personality disorders. In D. Lusk & T. L. Hayes (Eds.), *Overcoming bad leadership in organizations* (pp. 51–75). Oxford University Press.

Furnham, A., Richards, S. C., & Paulhus, D. L. (2013). The dark triad of personality: A 10-year review. *Social and Personality Psychology Compass, 7*(3), 199–216.

Gallese, V. (2001). The 'shared manifold' hypothesis: From mirror neurons to empathy. *Journal of Consciousness Studies, 8*(5–7), 33–50.

George, F. R., & Short, D. (2018). The cognitive neuroscience of narcissism. *Journal of Brain, Behavior and Cognitive Sciences, 1*(1), 1–9.

Gerdes, K. E., Segal, E. A., Jackson, K. F., & Mullins, J. L. (2011). Teaching empathy: A framework rooted in social cognitive neuroscience and social justice. *Journal of Social Work Education, 47*(1), 109–131.

Germain, M. L. (2018). *Narcissism at work: Personality disorders of corporate leaders.* Palgrave Macmillan.

Germain, M. L. (2023). Narcissistic leadership through the COVID-19 pandemic: The importance of empathy for leadership effectiveness. In D. McGuire & M. L. Germain (Eds.), *Leadership in a post-covid pandemic world* (pp. 73–93). de Gruyter. https://doi.org/10.1515/9783110799101-005

Goldenfeld, N., Baron-Cohen, S., & Wheelwright, S. (2005). Empathizing and systemizing in males, females, and autism. *Clinical Neuropsychiatry, 2*(6), 338–345.

Goleman, D. (2006). *Social intelligence: The new science of human relationships.* Bantam Books.

Goleman, D., & Boyatzis, R. (2017). Emotional intelligence has 12 elements. Which do you need to work on? *Harvard Business Review, 84*(2), 1–5.

Grijalva, E., Harms, P. D., Newman, D. A., Gaddis, B. H., & Fraley, R. C. (2015). Narcissism and leadership: A meta-analytic review of linear and nonlinear relationships. *Personnel Psychology, 68,* 1–47. https://doi.org/10.1111/peps.12072

Gudmundsson, A., & Southey, G. (2011). Leadership and the rise of the corporate psychopath: What can business schools do about the 'snakes inside'? *e-Journal of Social and Behavioural Research in Business, 2*(2), 18–27. https://eprints.qut.edu.au/48348/22/Gudmundsson.pdf. Accessed 20 February 2024.

Hare, R. D., & Neumann, C. S. (2008). Psychopathy as a clinical and empirical construct. *Annual Review of Clinical Psychology, 4,* 217–246. https://doi.org/10.1146/annurev.clinpsy.3.022806.091452

Heym, N., Kibowski, F., Bloxsom, C. A. J., Blanchard, A., Harper, A., Wallace, L., Firth, J., & Sumich, A. (2021). The dark empath: Characterizing dark traits in the presence of empathy. *Personality and Individual Differences, 169,* 110172.

Homer, A., & Fredericks, S. (2005). An empirical and theoretical exploration of disconnections between leadership and ethics. *Journal of Business Ethics, 59,* 233–246.

Hougaard, R., & Carter, J. (2022). *Compassionate leadership: How to do hard things in a human way.* Harvard Business Press.

Hoyk, R., & Hersey, P. (2008). *The ethical executive: Becoming aware of the root causes of unethical behavior: 45 psychological traps that every one of us falls prey to.* Stanford University Press.

Itzkowitz, S. (2020). Psychopathy and human evil: An overview. In S. Itzkowitz & E. F. Howell (Eds.), *Psychoanalysts, psychologists and psychiatrists discuss psychopathy and human evil* (pp. 13–37). Routledge.

Itzkowitz, S., & Howell, E. F. (2020). Introduction. In S. Itzkowitz & E. F. Howell (Eds.), *Psychoanalysts, psychologists and psychiatrists discuss psychopathy and human evil* (pp. 1–12). Routledge.

Jakobwitz, S., & Egan, V. (2006). The dark triad and normal personality traits. *Personality and Individual Differences, 40*(2), 331–339. https://doi.org/10.1016/j.paid.2005.07.006

James, S., Kavanagh, P. S., Jonason, P. K., Chonody, J. M., & Scrutton, H. E. (2014). The Dark Triad, schadenfreude, and sensational interests: Dark personalities, dark emotions, and dark behaviors. *Personality and Individual Differences, 68*, 211–216. https://doi.org/10.1016/j-Paid.2014.04.020

Jankowiak-Siuda, K., & Zajkowski, W. (2013). A neural model of mechanisms of empathy deficits in narcissism. *Medical Science Monitor: International Medical Journal of Experimental and Clinical Research, 19*, 934–941. https://doi.org/10.12659/MSM.889593

Jonason, P. K., & Krause, L. (2013). The emotional deficits associated with the Dark Triad traits: Cognitive empathy, affective empathy, and alexithymia. *Personality and individual Differences, 55*(5), 532–537.

Johnson, R. E., Silverman, S. B., Shyamsunder, A., Swee, H. Y., Rodopman, O. B., Cho, E., & Bauer, J. (2010). Acting superior but actually inferior? Correlates and consequences of workplace arrogance. *Human Performance, 23*(5), 403–427. https://doi.org/10.1080/08959285.2010.515279

Jonason, P. K., Slomski, S., & Partyka, J. (2012). The Dark Triad at work: How toxic employees get their way. *Personality and Individual Differences, 52*(3), 449–453.

Jonason, P. K., Lyons, M., Bethell, E. J., & Ross, R. (2013). Different routes to limited empathy in the sexes: Examining the links between the Dark Triad and empathy. *Personality and Individual Differences, 54*(5), 572–576.

Jonason, P. K., Żemojtel-Piotrowska, M., Piotrowski, J., Sedikides, C., Campbell, W. K., Gebauer, J. E., Maltby, J., Adamovic, M., Adams, B. G., Kadiyono, A. L., Atitsogbe, K. A., Bundhoo, H. Y., Bălțătescu, S., Bilić, S., Brulin, J. G., Chobthamkit, P., Del Carmen Dominguez, A., Dragova-Koleva, S., El-Astal, S., … Yahiiaev, I. (2020). Country-level correlates of the dark triad traits in 49 countries. *Journal of Personality, 88*(6), 1252–1267.

Jones, D. N., & Paulhus, D. L. (2009). Machiavellianism. In M. R. Leary, & R. H. Hoyle (Eds), *Handbook of individual differences in social behavior* (pp. 102–120). Guilford.

Jones, D. N., & Paulhus, D. L. (2010). Different provocations trigger aggression in narcissists and psychopaths. *Social Psychological and Personality Science, 1*(1), 12–18. https://doi.org/10.1177/1073191113514514105

Jones, D. N., & Paulhus, D. L. (2014). Introducing the short dark triad (SD3) a brief measure of dark personality traits. *Assessment, 21*(1), 28–41. https://doi.org/10.1177/1073191113514105

Jones, D. N., & Figueredo, A. J. (2013). The core of darkness: Uncovering the heart of the dark triad. *European Journal of Personality, 27*, 521–531. https://doi.org/10.1002/per.1893

Jones, D. N., & Neria, A. L. (2015). The Dark Triad and dispositional aggression. *Personality and Individual Differences, 86*, 360–364. https://doi.org/10.1016/j.paid.2015.06.021

Judge, T. A., Piccolo, R. F., & Kosalka, T. (2009). The bright and dark sides of leader traits: A review and theoretical extension of the leader trait paradigm. *The Leadership Quarterly, 20*(6), 855–875.

Jung, C. J. (1989). *Memories, dreams, reflections* (A. Jaffia, Ed., R. Winston & C. Winston, Trans.). Vintage.

Kaiser, R. B., & Hogan, R. (2007). The dark side of discretion: Leader personality and organizational decline. In R. Hooijberg, J. G. Hunt, J. Antonakis, K. B. Boal, & N. Lane (Eds.), *Be there even when you are not* (pp. 173–193). Emerald Group Publishing Limited.

Kaiser, R. B., LeBreton, J. M., & Hogan, J. (2015). The dark side of personality and extreme leader behavior. *Applied Psychology, 64*(1), 55–92.

Kets de Vries, M. F. R. (2014). Coaching the toxic leader. *Harvard Business Review, 92*(4), 100–109.

LeBreton, J. M., Shiverdecker, L. K., & Grimaldi, E. M. (2018). The dark triad and workplace behavior. *Annual Review of Organizational Psychology and Organizational Behavior, 5*, 387–414.

Leckelt, M., Küfner, A. C., Nestler, S., & Back, M. D. (2015). Behavioral processes underlying the decline of narcissists' popularity over time. *Journal of Personality and Social Psychology, 109*(5), 856–871. https://doi.org/10.1037/pspp0000057

Leslie, J. B. (2022). The dark side and leader derailment. In D. Lusk & T. L. Hayes (Eds.), *Overcoming bad leadership in organizations* (pp. 139–158). Oxford University Press.

Li, C., Murad, M., Shahzad, F., Khan, M. A. S., & Ashraf, S. F. (2020). Dark tetrad personality traits and counterproductive work behavior among doctors in Pakistan. *The International Journal of Health Planning and Management, 35*(5), 1173–1192. https://doi.org/10.1002/hpm.3025

Lilienfeld, S. O., Latzman, R. D., Watts, A. L., Smith, S. F., & Dutton, K. (2014). Correlates of psychopathic personality traits in everyday life: Results from a large community survey. *Frontiers in Psychology, 5*(740), 1–11.

Lipman-Blumen, J. (2005). The allure of toxic leaders: Why followers rarely escape their clutches. *Ivey Business Journal, 69*(3), 1–40.

Linton, D. K., & Power, J. L. (2013). The personality traits of workplace bullies are often shared by their victims: Is there a dark side to victims? *Personality and Individual Differences, 54*(6), 38–743. https://doi.org/10.1016/j.paid.2012.11.026

Lorenz, A. R., & Newman, J. P. (2002). Deficient response modulation and emotion processing in low-anxious Caucasian psychopathic offenders: Results from a lexical decision task. *Emotion, 2*(2), 91–104.

Luo, Y. L., Kovas, Y., Wang, L., Stalikas, A., Kyriazos, T. A., Gianniou, F. M., ... & Papageorgiou, K. A. (2023). Sex differences in the Dark Triad are sensitive to socioeconomic conditions: the adaptive value of narcissism in the UK, Greece, and China. *Current Psychology, 42*(26), 22436–22448.

Lynam, D. R., Gaughan, E. T., Miller, J. D., Mullins-Sweatt, & Widiger, T. A. (2010). Assessing basic traits associated with psychopathy: Development and validation of the elemental psychopathy assessment. *Psychological Assessment, 23*(1), 108–124. https://doi.org/10.1037/aOO21146

Ma, G. X., Born, M. P., Petrou, P., & Bakker, A. B. (2021). Bright sides of dark personality? A cross-cultural study on the dark triad and work outcomes. *International Journal of Selection and Assessment, 29*(3–4), 510–518. https://doi.org/10.1111/ijsa.12342

Maccoby, M. (2000). Narcissistic leaders: The incredible pros, the inevitable cons. *Harvard Business Review, 78*(1), 69–77.

Martin, S. R., Cote, S., & Woodruff, T. (2016). Echoes of our upbringing: How growing up wealthy or poor relates to narcissism, leader behavior, and leader effectiveness. *Academy of Management Journal, 59*(6), 2157–2177. https://doi.org/10.5465/amj.2015.0680

Maslow, A. (1970). *Motivation and personality* (2nd ed.). Harper and Row.

Mathieu, C., & Babiak, P. (2015). Tell me who you are, I'll tell you how you lead: Beyond the Full-Range Leadership Model, the role of corporate psychopathy on employee attitudes. *Personality and Individual Differences, 87*, 8–12. https://doi.org/10.1016/j.paid.2015.07.016

Mathieu, C., & Babiak, P. (2016a). Validating the B-Scan Self: A self-report measure of psychopathy in the workplace. *International Journal of Selection and Assessment, 24*(3), 272–284. https://doi.org/10.1111/ijsa.12146

Mathieu, C., & Babiak, P. (2016b). Workplace harassment: The influence of corporate psychopathy and the HEXACO model of personality. *Personality and Individual Differences, 101*, 298. https://doi.org/10.1016/j.paid.2016.05.225

Mathieu, C., Hare, R. D., Jones, D. N., Babiak, P., & Neumann, C. S. (2013). Factor structure of the B-Scan 360: A measure of corporate psychopathy. *Psychological Assessment, 25*(1), 288, 1–6. https://doi.org/10.1037/a0029262

Mathieu, C., Neumann, C. S., Hare, R. D., & Babiak, P. (2014). A dark side of leadership: Corporate psychopathy and its influence on employee well-being and job satisfaction. *Personality and Individual Differences, 59*, 83–88.

McCullough, J. (2022, March 18). *The psychopathic CEO.* https://www.forbes.com/sites/jackmccullough/2019/12/09/the-psychopathic-ceo/. Accessed 31 October 2024.

Mendez, M. F. (2009). The neurobiology of moral behavior: Review and neuropsychiatric implications. *CNS Spectrums, 14*(11), 608–620.

Merriam-Webster. (2014). *Miriam-Webster online dictionary*. http://www.mer riam-webster.com. Accessed 4 July 2024.

Moshagen, M., Hilbig, B. E., & Zettle, I. (2018). The dark core of personality. *Psychological Review, 125*(5), 656–688. https://doi.org/10.1037/rev 0000111

Mullins-Sweatt, S. N., Glover, N. G., Derefinko, K. J., Miller, J. D., & Widiger, T. A. (2010). The search for the successful psychopath. *Journal of Research in Personality, 44*(4), 554–558.

Muris, P., Merckelbach, H., Otgaar, H., & Meijer, E. (2017). The malevolent side of human nature: A meta-analysis and critical review of the literature on the dark triad (narcissism, Machiavellianism, and psychopathy). *Perspectives on Psychological Science, 12*(2), 183–204.

Neumann, C. C., & Hare, R. D. (2008). Psychopathic traits in a large community sample: Links to violence, alcohol use, and intelligence. *Journal of Consulting and Clinical Psychology, 76*(5), 893–899. https://doi.org/10.1037/0022-006X.76.5.893

Ong, C. W., Roberts, R., Arthur, C. A., Woodman, T., & Akehurst, S. (2016). The leader ship is sinking: A temporal investigation of narcissistic leadership. *Journal of Personality, 84*(2), 237–247. https://doi.org/10.1111/jopy.12155

Pajevic, M., Vukosavljevic-Gvozden, T., Stevanovic, N., & Neumann, C. S. (2018). The relationship between the Dark Tetrad and a two-dimensional view of empathy. *Personality and Individual Differences, 123*, 125–130. https://doi.org/10.1016/j.paid.2017.11.009

Patrick, C. J. (2018). Cognitive and emotional processing in psychopathy. In C. J. Patrick (Ed.), *Handbook of psychopathy* (2nd ed., pp. 422–455). Guilford Press.

Paulhus, D. L. (2014). Toward a taxonomy of dark personalities. *Current Directions in Psychological Science, 23*(6), 421–426.

Paulhus, D. L., & Williams, K. M. (2002). The dark triad of personality: Narcissism, Machiavellianism, and psychopathy. *Journal of Research in Personality, 36*(6), 556–563.

Penney, L. M., & Spector, P. E. (2002). Narcissism and counterproductive work behavior: Do bigger egos mean bigger problems? *International Journal of Selection and Assessment, 10*(1–2), 126–134. https://doi.org/10.1111/1468-2389.00199

Pilch, I., & Turska, E. (2015). Relationships between Machiavellianism, organizational culture, and workplace bullying: Emotional abuse from the target's and the perpetrator's perspective. *Journal of Business Ethics, 128*, 83–93. https://doi.org/10.1007/s10551-014-2081-3

Pincus, A. L., Ansell, E. B., Pimentel, C. A., Cain, N. M., Wright, A. G., & Levy, K. N. (2009). Initial construction and validation of the Pathological

Narcissism Inventory. *Psychological Assessment, 21*(3), 365–379. https://doi.org/10.1037/a0016530

Porter, S., ten Brinke, L., Baker, A., & Wallace, B. (2011). Would I lie to you? "Leakage" in deceptive facial expressions relates to psychopathy and emotional intelligence. *Personality and Individual Differences, 51*(2), 133–137.

Preston, S. D., & de Waal, F. B. M. (2002). Empathy: Its ultimate and proximate bases. *Behavioral and Brain Sciences, 25*(1), 1–20. https://doi.org/10.1017/S0140525X02000018

O'Boyle, E. H., Jr., Forsyth, D. R., Banks, G. C., & McDaniel, M. A. (2012). A meta-analysis of the Dark Triad and work behavior: A social exchange perspective. *Journal of Applied Psychology, 97*, 557–579.

Orange exec's guilty verdicts over worker suicides upheld by appeals court. (2022, September, 30). Reuters.com. https://www.reuters.com/markets/europe/orange-execs-guilty-verdicts-over-worker-suicides-upheld-by-appeal-court-2022-09-30/. Accessed 21 February 2024.

Ramos-Vera, C., O'Diana, A. G., Villena, A. S., Bonfá-Araujo, B., de Oliveira Barros, L., Noronha, A. P. P., Gómez-Acosta, A., Sierra-Barón, W., Gerymski, R., Ogundokun, R. O., Babatunde, A. N., Abdulahi, A. R. T., & Adeniyi, E. A. (2023). Dark and light triad: A cross-cultural comparison of network analysis in 5 countries. *Personality and Individual Differences, 215*, 112377. https://doi.org/10.1016/j.paid.2023.112377

Raskin, R. N., & Hall, C. S. (1979). A narcissistic personality inventory. *Psychological Reports, 45*(2), 590–590. https://doi.org/10.2466/PM.1979.45.2.590

Rauthmann, J. F., & Kolar, G. P. (2012). How "dark" are the Dark Triad traits? Examining the perceived darkness of narcissism, Machiavellianism, and psychopathy. *Personality and Individual Differences, 53*(7), 884–889. https://doi.org/10.1016/j.paid.2012.06.020

Reed, S. F. (1994). *The toxic executive: A step-by-step guide for turning your boss (or yourself) from noxious to nurturing.* Harper Business.

Riaz, A., Batool, S., & SAAD, M. S. (2019). The missing link between high performance work practices and perceived organizational politics. *Revista de Administração de Empresas, 59*, 82–94. https://doi.org/10.1590/s0034-759020190202

Ricks, J., & Fraedrich, J. (1999). The paradox of Machiavellianism: Machiavellianism may make for productive sales but poor management reviews. *Journal of Business Ethics, 20*(3), 197.

Rifkin, J. (2009). *The empathic civilization.* Tarcher.

Robertson, S. A., Datu, J. A. D., Brawley, A. M., Pury, C. L., & Mateo, N. J. (2016). The Dark Triad and social behavior: The influence of self-construal and power distance. *Personality and Individual Differences, 98*, 69–74. https://doi.org/10.1016/j.paid.2016.03.090

Rogoza, R., Żemojtel-Piotrowska, M., Jonason, P. K., Piotrowski, J., Campbell, K. W., Gebauer, J., & Wlodarczyk, A. (2021). Structure of dark triad dirty dozen across eight world regions. *Assessment, 28*(4), 1125–1135. https://doi.org/10.1177/1073191120922611

Ronson, J. (2012). *The psychopath test: A journey through the madness industry*. Riverhead Books.

Rosenthal, S. A., & Pittinsky, T. L. (2006). Narcissistic leadership. *The Leadership Quarterly, 17*(6), 617–633.

Rotolo, C. T., & Bracken, D. W. (2022). Assessing the dark side: Making informed decisions throughout the leadership lifecycle. In D. Lusk & T. L. Hayes (Eds.), *Overcoming bad leadership in organizations* (pp. 277–324). Oxford University Press.

Sakalaki, M., Richardson, C., & Thépaut, Y. (2007). Machiavellianism and economic opportunism. *Journal of Applied Social Psychology, 37*(6), 1181–1190. https://doi.org/10.1111/j.1559-1816.2007.00208.x

Sanecka, E. (2013). The effects of supervisors' subclinical psychopathy on subordinates' organizational commitment, job satisfaction and satisfaction with supervisor. *The Journal of Education, Culture, and Society, 4*(2), 172–191.

Schyns, B., Gauglitz, I. K., Wisse, B., & Schütz, A. (2022). How to mitigate destructive leadership: Human resources practices that mitigate dark triad leaders' destructive tendencies. In D. Lusk & T. L. Hayes (Eds.), *Overcoming bad leadership in organizations* (pp. 251–274). Oxford University Press. https://doi.org/10.1093/050/9780197552759.003.0013

Schyns, B., Wisse, B., & Sanders, S. (2019). Shady strategic behavior: Recognizing strategic followership of Dark Triad followers. *Academy of Management Perspectives, 33*(2), 234–249. https://doi.org/10.5465/amp.2017.0005

Schurz, M., Radua, J., Tholen, M. G., Maliske, L., Margulies, D. S., Mars, R. B., Sallet, J., & Kanske, P. (2021). Toward a hierarchical model of social cognition: A neuroimaging meta-analysis and integrative review of empathy and theory of mind. *Psychological Bulletin, 147*(3), 293–327. https://doi.org/10.1037/bul0000303

Schofield, H. (2019, July 11). *France Telecom bullying trial sheds light on spate of suicides*. BBC.com. https://www.bbc.com/news/world-europe-48948776. Accessed 21 February 2024.

Seara-Cardoso, A., Neumann, C., Roiser, J., McCrory, E., & Viding, E. (2012). Investigating associations between empathy, morality and psychopathic personality traits in the general population. *Personality and Individual Differences, 52*(1), 67–71.

Sedikides, C., & Campbell, W. K. (2017). Narcissistic force meets systemic resistance: The energy clash model. *Perspectives on Psychological Science, 12*(3), 400–421. https://doi.org/10.1177/1745691617692105

Shoemaker, W. J. (2012). The social brain network and human moral behavior. *Zygon, 47*(4), 806–820.

Simmons, L. (2020, April 30). *How narcissistic leaders destroy from within.* https://www.gsb.stanford.edu/insights/how-narcissistic-leaders-destroy-within. Accessed 3 March 2024.

Smith, A. (2006). Cognitive empathy and emotional empathy in human behavior and evolution. *The Psychological Record, 56*(1), 3–21.

Spain, S. M. (2019). *Leadership, work and the dark side of personality.* Academic Press.

Spain, S. M., Harms, P., & LeBreton, J. M. (2014). The dark side of personality at work. *Journal of Organizational Behavior, 35*(S1), S41–S60.

Spurk, D., Keller, A. C., & Hirschi, A. (2016). Do bad guys get ahead or fall behind? Relationships of the dark triad of personality with objective and subjective career success. *Social Psychological and Personality Science, 7*(2), 113–121.

Stern, R. J. (2021). Why bad leaders? A perspective from WICS. In A. Örtenblad (Ed.), *Debating bad leadership: Reasons and remedies* (pp. 154–165). Palgrave Macmillan.

Szabó, E., & Bereczkei, T. (2017). Different paths to different strategies? Unique associations among facets of the Dark Triad, empathy, and trait emotional intelligence. *Advances in Cognitive Psychology, 13*(4), 306–313. https://doi.org/10.5709/acp-0230-7

Thibault, T., & Kelloway, E. K. (2020). Personality and counterproductive work behavior. In B. J. Carducci, C. S. Nave, J. S. Mio, & R. E. Riggio (Eds.), *The Wiley encyclopedia of personality and individual differences: Clinical, applied, and cross-cultural research* (pp. 599–603). Wiley.

Tokarev, A., Phillips, A. R., Hughes, D. J., & Irwing, P. (2017). Leader dark traits, workplace bullying, and employee depression: Exploring mediation and the role of the dark core. *Journal of Abnormal Psychology, 126*(7), 911–920. https://doi.org/10.1037/abn0000199

Vernon, P. A., Villani, V. C., Vickers, L. C., & Harris, J. A. (2008). A behavioral genetic investigation of the Dark Triad and the Big 5. *Personality and Individual Differences, 44*(2), 445–452. https://doi.org/10.1016/j.paid.2007.09.007

Visser, B. A., & Doyle, L. A. (2022). HEXACO personality. In D. Lusk & T. L. Hayes (Eds.), *Overcoming bad leadership in organizations* (pp. 76–96). Oxford University Press.

Volmer, J., Koch, I. K., & Göritz, A. S. (2016). The bright and dark sides of leaders' dark triad traits: Effects on subordinates' career success and well-being. *Personality and Individual Differences, 101*, 413–418. https://doi.org/10.1016/j.paid2016.06.046

Vonk, J., Zeigler-Hill, V., Mayhew, P., & Mercer, S. (2013). Mirror, mirror on the wall, which form of narcissist knows self and others best of all? *Personality and Individual Differences, 54*(3), 396–401. https://doi.org/10.1016/j.paid.2012.10.010

Wai, M., & Tiliopoulos, N. (2012). The affective and cognitive empathic nature of the dark triad of personality. *Personality and Individual Differences, 52*(7), 794–799. https://doi.org/10.1016/j.paid.2012.01.008

Wakabayashi, A., Baron-Cohen, S., & Wheelwright, S. (2006). Individual and gender differences in empathizing and systemizing: Measurement of individual differences by the Empathy Quotient (EQ) and the Systemizing Quotient (SQ). *Shinrigaku Kenkyu: The Japanese Journal of Psychology, 77*(3), 271–277. https://doi.org/10.4992/jjpsy.77.271

Webster, V., Brough, P., & Daly, K. (2016). Fight, flight or freeze: Common responses for follower coping with toxic leadership. *Stress and Health, 32*(4), 346–354.

Westerlaken, K. M., & Woods, P. R. (2013). The relationship between psychopathy and the full range leadership model. *Personality and Individual Differences, 54*, 41–46.

Winter, S., Stylianou, A., & Giacalone, R. (2004). Individual differences in the acceptability of unethical information technology practices: The case of Machiavellianism and ethical ideology. *Journal of Business Ethics, 54*, 279–301.

Wood, J. D., & Liu, H. (2021). Failure in leadership: The deeper psychosocial currents. In A. Örtenblad (Ed.), *Debating bad leadership: Reasons and remedies* (pp. 182–204). Palgrave Macmillan.

Wood, J. D., Meister, A., & Liu, H. (2021). Defining the good, the bad, and the evil. In A. Örtenblad (Ed.), *Debating bad leadership: Reasons and remedies* (pp. 47–65). Palgrave Macmillan.

Wright, A. G., Pincus, A. L., Thomas, K. M., Hopwood, C. J., Markon, K. E., & Krueger, R. F. (2013). Conceptions of narcissism and the DSM-5 pathological personality traits. *Assessment, 20*(3), 339–352. https://doi.org/10.1177/1073191113486692

Bad Leader/Abusive Supervisor/Destructive Leader

Abstract This chapter describes the next bad leader on the spectrum, the abusive, destructive leader. This leader is not as bad as the dark triad leader and does not have a personality disorder. They are also known as petty tyrants and toxic leaders. They have more empathy than the dark triad, but not much. They still create poor outcomes for their subordinates and organizations, such as high turnover, and low organizational commitment, job satisfaction, and job performance.

Keywords Abusive supervision · Destructive leader · Petty tyrant

This leader does not have a personality disorder and is not considered to be in the dark triad. These leaders may yet be able to be developed into a better leader, as they still have some of their humanity left; they still have some empathy. These leaders would be on Baron-Cohen's (2011) Level 1 on the empathy curve, one level above zero degrees of negative empathy. This leader still hurts others but are able to feel regret because they are capable of self-reflection. However, they do not have enough self-control to stop their behavior; they don't have enough empathy to do so. Their empathy circuit goes down when their temper is triggered, or their judgment is clouded; they cannot feel others' feelings at that point. At this point they become abusive.

© The Author(s), under exclusive license to Springer Nature Switzerland AG 2025
B. W. Eversole, *The Leadership Spectrum*,
https://doi.org/10.1007/978-3-031-73557-8_3

While psychopaths tend to be abusive supervisors (Boddy et al., 2015; Mathieu & Babiak, 2016; Wisse & Sleebos, 2016), not all abusive supervisors are psychopaths. Narcissists tend not to be abusive supervisors (Nevicka et al., 2018; Wisse & Sleebos, 2016), unless subordinates had low self-esteem.

DEFINED

Also known as abusive supervisors (Tepper et al., 2017) or destructive leaders (Einarsen et al., 2007), these leaders treat their employees as a means to an end, rather than someone who they are trying to help be successful. Dark triad leaders are also destructive leaders and abusive supervisors, as leaders at the end of the spectrum encompass all the behaviors of leaders beneath them on the spectrum until the middle (incivility). Therefore, dark triad leaders are also destructive, ineffective and uncivil leaders, destructive leaders are also ineffective and uncivil leaders, and ineffective leaders are also uncivil leaders.

Tepper et al. (2017) defined abusive supervision as "the extent to which supervisors engage in the sustained display of hostile verbal- and non-verbal behaviors" (p. 178). Destructive leader behavior "is defined as the systematic and repeated behaviour by a leader, supervisor or manager that violates the legitimate interest of the organization by undermining and/or sabotaging the organization's goals, tasks, resources, and effectiveness and/or the motivation, well-being or job satisfaction of his/her subordinates" (Einarsen et al., 2007, p. 207). Silver et al. (2023) expanded their definition to include leaders who do not promote women employees due to discrimination.

TRAITS

Abusive supervisors tend to be preoccupied with the belief that they are different from others (Johnson et al., 2012; Tepper et al., 2011). Moreover, when supervisors feel that they have been treated unfairly by their company, they may tend to be abusive toward their direct reports (Hoobler & Brass, 2006). Leaders may also become abusive supervisors when their psychological resources become depleted (Byrne et al., 2014). Abusive supervisors have difficulty with self-regulation (Tepper et al., 2017). They are inconsiderate, rude, arrogant, and lose their temper easily (Bies, 2002).

In a recent study by Ikechukwu-Ifudu (2024), employees were asked what they considered bad leadership to be characterized by. They responded that lack of accountability and lack of transparency were the number one characteristics of bad leaders. These research results linking bad leadership with lack of accountability and transparency have also been reported in the literature (Gberevbie et al., 2017; Hall et al., 2017; Melo et al., 2020).

Behaviors

Abusive supervisors (Tepper et al., 2017) publicly ridicule their subordinates, blaming them inappropriately and undermining them in uncontrolled outbursts in sustained hostile acts. They tell their direct reports that their feelings or thoughts are stupid (Hoobler & Brass, 2006). They yell at direct reports and throw tantrums and objects (Tepper, 2000). They show hostility toward direct reports, using coercion and assuming guilt (Bies, 2002).

Destructive leader behaviors have to be both systematic and repeated, such as weekly over six months (Einarsen et al., 2007). They can include harassment, bullying, mistreatment, and incivility.

Also known as petty tyrant (Ashforth, 1994; Einarsen et al., 2007), these inconsiderate, arbitrary, egoistic leaders discourage initiative, belittle their direct reports while lording their powers over them and meting out meaningless punishments. They oppressively, vindictively, and capriciously use their power in a tyrannical and arbitrary manner (Ashforth, 1994, 1997, 2003). They use their authority in order to gain personally, and they are unfair and rude to direct reports (Ashforth, 1994).

Reed's (1994) toxic leaders would be equivalent to abusive supervisors and petty tyrants. According to Reed (1994), toxic leaders are "accusational, habitual liars, invalidate their direct reports, discredit others and their ideas, they are intentionally obtuse in meetings and misleading, they play favorites, they are jealous of peers, they collect power, and they are self-serving in making decisions" (p. 269).

Prevalence

In the U.S., abusive supervision affects an estimated 10% of U.S. workers (Tepper et al., 2017).

Outcomes

Abusive supervision is associated with low organizational commitment, job satisfaction, and job performance (Babiak & Hare, 2019; Tepper, 2000, 2007), abusive leaders increase their employees' intention to leave (Mathieu & Babiak, 2016; Tepper, 2000; Tepper et al., 2017), and they cost organizations an estimated $23.8 billion in the U.S. due to health care, absenteeism, and lost productivity every year (Tepper et al., 2006). Abusive supervision increases CWB (Tepper et al., 2017) and decreases OCB (Tepper, 2007). Those who work for abusive supervisors have less positive attitudes toward their jobs and their organizations and have increased psychological distress and decreased psychological health (Park et al., 2018; Tepper, 2000; Tepper et al., 2017). Abusive supervision also reduces the sharing of knowledge (Choi et al., 2019; Lee et al., 2018) and morale (Tepper et al., 2017).

Destructive leadership behaviors have been linked to reduced subordinate performance and well-being (Duffy et al., 2006; Hoobler & Brass, 2006; Zellars et al., 2002). They also reduce job satisfaction and motivation (Einarsen et al., 2007).

In Erickson et al.'s (2007) study, bad leaders made subordinates feel angry, reduced their self-esteem, and left them feeling frustrated. Subordinates felt a lack of motivation, a decrease in performance, and left the company as a result. Most striking of all was what happened to the bad leaders in the respondents' organizations—almost half of the respondents said the bad leader was promoted or rewarded, while 20% said nothing happened at all. Only 13% said the bad leader had been forced out. The authors contacted the employees who said they had left the company, calculated their salaries based on their titles, and at 2X their salaries, the turnover cost to their companies would have been over $3 million.

Gender and Abusive Supervision/ Destructive Leadership

"She's a bitch. He's having a bad day" (Yun & Shum, 2023, p. 3807).

Women who are abusive supervisors are judged more harshly for it (Kim et al., 2022). They are seen as less effective than men who are abusive supervisors due to role incongruity, since women are supposed to be caring and communal. Yun and Shum (2023) also found that employees make external attribution in the case of women abusive leaders (they attribute abuse to women leaders, rather than themselves, since they do not anticipate that women will be abusive), and therefore are insubordinate. Kim et al. (2022) also found that employees were more likely to form external attributions for women abusive leaders. Men are more likely to be abusive supervisors than women (Byrne et al., 2014; Eaton & Nevicka, 2022).

CULTURE AND ABUSIVE SUPERVISION/ DESTRUCTIVE LEADERSHIP

Most of the research on abusive supervision has been done in Western contexts (Tepper, 2000). Khan (2014) studied abusive supervision in different countries and concluded that it existed in virtually all national cultures although both the subordinate's perception and the force of that abuse differ by culture. Destructive leaders are about 11% in the Netherlands (Hubert & van Veldhoven, 2001) and around 30% in Norway (Aasland et al., 2010), where a third of workers reported that they have experienced destructive leaders often in the last six months.

Similarly, Palmer et al. (2024) studied destructive leadership in 12 countries and found that there were differences in the relationship between destructive leadership and the job satisfaction of subordinates. For example, as power distance and uncertainty avoidance increase, so does the negative relationship between destructive leadership and job satisfaction. For example, Rafferty and Restubog (2011) studied abusive supervision in the Philippines and found that the subordinates of abusive supervisors retaliated by withholding voluntary OCB and discretionary work effort. Stempel and Rigotti (2018) studied employees in Germany and found no differences between the scores for men and women as abusive supervisors.

Research has suggested that direct reports of abusive supervisors in cultures with high power distance (Hofstede, 1991), such as Taiwan or Singapore, are more accepting of the abuse than those from cultures with low power distance, such as the U.S. or Australia (Lian et al., 2012; Vogel et al, 2015). Zhang and Liao (2015) found that power distance moderated the relationship between abusive supervision and employee performance and behaviors in Asia. Abusive supervision in Taiwan causes considerable psychological distress in frontline employees (Hu, 2012). A study by Cahyono et al. (2020) in Indonesia showed that abusive supervisors reduced their subordinates' OCB. A similar study by Pradhan et al.

(2018) in India showed a strong relationship between abusive supervision and subordinates' turnover intention. Lu et al. (2012) compared Chinese destructive leadership behavior with Einarsen et al.'s (2007) definition.

van Niekerk (2013) found that destructive leadership was related to psychological distress in a South African study. Saleem et al. (2024) found that work stress was an important antecedent for abusive supervision, more so for women leaders than men, in their Pakistani study. Shaw et al. (2015) found similar results for destructive leader behavior in Australian, American, and Iranian samples.

CONCLUSION

Bad leaders such as abusive supervisors and destructive leaders do not have personality disorders, but subject their subordinates to mistreatment, nevertheless. They have a little more empathy than the dark triad leaders, but they still do not treat their employees very well, leading to poor outcomes such as increased turnover and reduced performance. The next level on the spectrum are leaders who are ineffective and who bully their subordinates.

REFERENCES

Aasland, M. S., Skogstad, A., Notelaers, G., Nielsen, M. B., & Einarsen, S. (2010). The prevalence of destructive leadership behaviour. *British Journal of Management, 21,* 438–452.

Ashforth, B. E. (1994). Petty tyranny in organizations. *Human Relations, 47,* 755–778. https://doi.org/10.1177/001872679404700701

Ashforth, B. E. (1997). Petty tyranny in organizations: A preliminary examination of antecedents and consequences. *Canadian Journal of Administrative Sciences/revue Canadienne des Sciences de l'Administration, 14*(2), 126–140.

Ashforth, B. E. (2003). Petty tyranny. In L. W. Porter, H. L. Angle, & R. W. Allen (Eds.), *Organizational influence processes* (pp. 151–171). M. E. Sharpe.

Babiak, P., & Hare, R. D. (2019). *Snakes in suits* (2nd ed.). Harper Business.

Baron-Cohen, S. (2011). *The science of evil: On empathy and the origins of cruelty.* Basic Books.

Bies, R. J. (2002). Interactional (in) justice: The sacred and the profane. In J. Greenberg & R. Cropanzano (Eds.), *Advances in organizational justice* (pp. 89–118). Stanford Business Books.

Boddy, C., Miles, D., Sanyal, C., & Hartog, M. (2015). Extreme managers, extreme workplaces: Capitalism, organizations and corporate psychopaths.

Organization, 22(4), 530–551. https://doi.org/10.1177/135050841557 2508

Byrne, A., Dionisi, A. M., Barling, J., Akers, A., Robertson, J., Lys, R., Wylie, J., & Dupré, K. (2014). The depleted leader: The influence of leaders' diminished psychological resources on leadership behaviors. *The Leadership Quarterly, 25*(2), 344–357.

Cahyono, E., Haryono, T., Haryanto, B., & Harsono, M. (2020). The role of gender in the relationship between abusive supervision and employee's organisational citizenship behaviour in Indonesia. *International Journal of Trade and Global Markets, 13*(3), 311–322.

Choi, W., Kim, S. L., & Yun, S. (2019). A social exchange perspective of abusive supervision and knowledge sharing: Investigating the moderating effects of psychological contract fulfillment and self-enhancement motive. *Journal of Business and Psychology, 34*, 305–319. https://doi.org/10.1007/s10869-018-9542-0

Duffy, M. K., Ganster, D. C., Shaw, J. D., Johnson, J. L., & Pagon, M. (2006). The social context of undermining behavior at work. *Organizational Behavior and Human Decision Processes, 101*(1), 105–126. https://doi.org/10.1016/j.obhdp.2006.04.005

Eaton, A. A., & Nevicka, B. (2022). Gender and the dark side of leadership. In D. Lusk & T. L. Hayes (Eds.), *Overcoming bad leadership in organizations* (pp. 176–197). Oxford University Press.

Einarsen, S., Aasland, M. S., & Skogstad, A. (2007). Destructive leadership behaviour: A definition and conceptual model. *The Leadership Quarterly, 18*, 207–216.

Gberevbie, D., Joshua, S., Excellence-Oluye, N., & Oyeyemi, A. (2017). Accountability for sustainable development and the challenges of leadership in Nigeria, 1999–2015. *SAGE Open, 7*(4), 2158244017742951.

Hall, A. T., Frink, D. D., & Buckley, M. R. (2017). An accountability account: A review and synthesis of the theoretical and empirical research on felt accountability. *Journal of Organizational Behaviour, 38*(2), 204–224.

Hofstede, G. (1991). *Cultures and organizations: Software of the mind.* McGraw-Hill.

Hoobler, J. M., & Brass, D. J. (2006). Abusive supervision and family undermining as displaced aggression. *Journal of Applied Psychology, 91*, 1125–1133.

Hu, H. H. (2012). The influence of employee emotional intelligence on coping with supervisor abuse in a banking context. *Social Behavior and Personality: An International Journal, 40*(5), 863–874. https://doi.org/10.2224/sbp.2012.40.5.863

Hubert, A. B., & van Veldhoven, M. J. P. M. (2001). Risk sectors for undesirable behaviour and mobbing. *European Journal of Work and Organizational Psychology, 10*, 415–424.

Ikechukwu-Ifudu, V. (2024). Unraveling the paradox: The persistence of bad leadership. *Presented at the University Forum of Human Resource Development Conference*, June 12–14, 2014, Lisbon, Portugal.

Johnson, R. E., Venus, M., Lanaj, K., Mao, C., & Chang, C. H. (2012). Leader identity as an antecedent of the frequency and consistency of transformational, consideration, and abusive leadership behaviors. *Journal of Applied Psychology*, 97(6), 1262.

Khan, S. N. (2014). Impact of Hofstede's cultural dimensions on subordinate's perception of abusive supervision. *International Journal of Business and Management*, 9(12), 239–251.

Kim, J. K., Harold, C. M., & Holtz, B. C. (2022). Evaluations of abusive supervisors: The moderating role of the abuser's gender. *Journal of Organizational Behavior*, 43(3), 465–482. https://doi.org/10.1002/job.2581

Lee, S., Kim, S. L., & Yun, S. (2018). A moderated mediation model of the relationship between abusive supervision and knowledge sharing. *The Leadership Quarterly*, 29(3), 403–413.

Lian, H., Ferris, D. L., & Brown, D. J. (2012). Does power distance exacerbate or mitigate the effects of abusive supervision? It depends on the outcome. *Journal of Applied Psychology*, 97(1), 107–123. https://doi.org/10.1037/a0024610

Lu, H., Ling, W., Wu, Y., & Liu, Y. (2012). A Chinese perspective on the content and structure of destructive leadership. *Chinese Management Studies*, 6(2), 271–283.

Mathieu, C., & Babiak, P. (2016). Corporate psychopathy and abusive supervision: Their influence on employees' job satisfaction and turnover intentions. *Personality and Individual Differences*, 91, 102–106. https://doi.org/10.1016/j.paid.2015.12.0020191-8869

Melo, P. N., Martins, A., & Pereira, M. (2020). The relationship between leadership and accountability: A review and synthesis of the research. *Journal of Entrepreneurship Education*, 23(6), 1–10.

Nevicka, B., De Hoogh, A. H., Den Hartog, D. N., & Belschak, F. D. (2018). Narcissistic leaders and their victims: Followers low on self-esteem and low on core self-evaluations suffer most. *Frontiers in Psychology*, 9, 315700. https://doi.org/10.3389/fpsyg2018.00422

Palmer, J. C., Mackey, J. D., McAllister, C. P., Alexander, K. C., Phillipich, M. A., Mercer, I. S., & Ellen III, B. P. (2024). Cultural values as moderators of the relationship between destructive leadership and followers' job satisfaction. *Group & Organization Management*, 10596011241232559.

Park, J. H., Carter, M. Z., DeFrank, R. S., & Deng, Q. (2018). Abusive supervision, psychological distress, and silence: The effects of gender dissimilarity between supervisors and subordinates. *Journal of Business Ethics*, 153, 775–792.

Pradhan, S., Jena, L. K., & Mohapatra, M. (2018). Role of gender on the relationship between abusive supervision and employee's intention to quit in Indian electricity distribution companies. *Gender in Management: An International Journal, 33*(4), 282–295.

Rafferty, A. E., & Restubog, S. L. D. (2011). The influence of abusive supervisors on followers' organizational citizenship behaviours: The hidden costs of abusive supervision. *British Journal of Management, 22*(2), 270–285. https://doi.org/10.1111/j.1467-8551.2010.00732.x

Reed, S. F. (1994). *The toxic executive: A step-by-step guide for turning your boss (or yourself) from noxious to nurturing.* Harper Business.

Saleem, S., Sajid, M., Arshad, M., Raziq, M. M., & Shaheen, S. (2024). Work stress, ego depletion, gender and abusive supervision: A self-regulatory perspective. *The Service Industries Journal, 44*(5–6), 391–411.

Shaw, J. B., Erickson, A., & Nasirzadeh, F. (2015). Destructive leader behavior: A comparison of Australian, American, and Iranian leaders using the Destructive Leadership Questionnaire. *International Journal of Cross Cultural Management, 15*(3), 329–345. https://doi.org/10.1177/147059 5815606740

Silver, E. R., King, D. D., & Hebl, M. (2023). Social inequalities in leadership: Shifting the focus from deficient followers to destructive leaders. *Management Decision, 61*(4), 959–974. https://doi.org/10.1108/MD-06-2021-0809

Stempel, C. R., & Rigotti, T. (2018). Leaders' gender, perceived abusive supervision and health. *Frontiers in Psychology, 9*, 2427. https://doi.org/10.3389/fpsyg.2018.02427

Tepper, B. J. (2000). Consequences of abusive supervision. *Academy of Management Journal, 43*(2), 178–190. https://doi.org/10.2307/1556375

Tepper, B. J. (2007). Abusive supervision in work organizations: Review synthesis, and research agenda. *Journal of Management, 33*, 261–289.

Tepper, B., Duffy, M. K., Henle, C. A., & Lambert, L. S. (2006). Procedural injustice, victim precipitation, and abusive supervision. *Personnel Psychology, 59*(1), 101–123. https://doi.org/10.1111/j.1744-6570.2006.00725.x

Tepper, B. J., Moss, S. E., & Duffy, M. K. (2011). Predictors of abusive supervision: Supervisor perceptions of deep-level dissimilarity, relationship conflict, and subordinate performance. *Academy of Management Journal, 54*, 279–294.

Tepper, B. J., Simon, L., & Park, H. M. (2017). Abusive supervision. *Annual Review of Organizational Psychology and Organizational Behavior, 4*(1), 123–152. https://doi.org/10.1146/annurev-orgpsych-041015-062539

Tepper, B. J., Simon, L., & Park, H. M. (2017). Abusive supervision. *Annual Review of Organizational Psychology and Organizational Behavior, 4*(1), 123–152. https://doi.org/10.1146/annurev-orgpsych-041015-062539

van Niekerk, A. (2013). *The relationship between destructive leadership and psychological distress in South African organizations: The moderating effect of gender*. Available from ProQuest Dissertations & Theses A&I; ProQuest Dissertations & Theses Global (2901810357).

Vogel, R. M., Mitchell, M. S., Tepper, B. J., Restubog, S. L., Hu, C., Hua, W., & Huang, J. C. (2015). A cross-cultural examination of subordinates' perceptions of and reactions to abusive supervision. *Journal of Organizational Behavior, 36*(5), 720–745. https://doi.org/10.1002/job.1984

Wisse, B., & Sleebos, E. (2016). When the dark ones gain power: Perceived position power strengthens the effect of supervisor Machiavellianism on abusive supervision in work teams. *Personality and Individual Differences, 99*, 122–126.

Yun, D., & Shum, C. (2023). An attribution account of the effects of leaders' gender and abusive supervision on employee insubordination. *International Journal of Contemporary Hospitality Management, 35*(11), 3807–3824.

Zellars, K. L., Tepper, B. J., & Duffy, M. K. (2002). Abusive supervision and subordinates' organizational citizenship behavior. *Journal of Applied Psychology, 87*, 1068–1076. https://doi.org/10.1037//0021-9010.87.6.1068

Zhang, Y., & Liao, Z. (2015). Consequences of abusive supervision: A meta-analytic review. *Asia Pacific Journal of Management, 32*, 959–987. https://doi.org/10.1007/s10490-015-9425-0

CHAPTER 4

Ineffective, Bullying Leaders

Abstract This chapter describes leaders who are ineffective as supervisors and who can also be bullies to their subordinates. They can also be described as sub-toxic, as their behavior does not rise to the level of toxic leader. These leaders do have some empathy which keeps them from being more harmful. These leaders have poor outcomes for their subordinates. Bullying direct and indirect costs are over $40 billion annually to U.S. organizations (Porter et al., Employee Responsibilities and Rights Journal 30:119–141, 2018).

Keywords Ineffective supervisors · Workplace bullies

This is the ineffective leader who does a poor job of managing subordinates. These leaders are sub-toxic (Reed, 1994), and exhibit behaviors that are harmful and ineffective in managing their direct reports. Many leaders fall into this category as they have not been trained in how to be a good supervisor and end up with very bad habits in managing their subordinates.

Ineffective leaders would be at Level 2 of empathy (Baron-Cohen, 2011) and would have enough empathy to stop them from physically harming others. They can still shout at direct reports, saying hurtful things, but they are not as bad as abusive supervisors and destructive leaders.

DEFINED

Ineffective leader behavior is made up of below standard performance on normal, everyday tasks rather than conspicuously "bad" behaviors such as performed by abusive supervisors or the dark triad (Patel et al., 2022). In the case of leaders, it would be the everyday task of supervising subordinates. The Workplace Bullying Institute (WBI, 2021). defines bullying as "repeated mistreatment, abusive conduct, that is threatening, intimidating, humiliating, work sabotage or verbal abuse." It is a form of aggression which occurs frequently with extended exposure and many different behaviors, and can escalate (Keashly, 2012).

TRAITS

Workplace bullies tend to have certain personality traits such as anger (Hershcovis et al., 2007), anxiety (Fox & Spector, 1999) and vengefulness (Douglas & Martinko, 2001). Bullies have often been bullied themselves (Hauge et al., 2009) and also have lower self-esteem (Ferris et al., 2011, 2012).

BEHAVIORS

According to Hamlin et al. (2012) an ineffective supervisor exhibits the following behaviors: "poor planning, organizing and controlling, bad judgment, low standards and/or tolerance of poor performance from others; shows lack of interest in or respect for staff, and/ or care or concern for their welfare or well-being; inappropriate autocratic, dictatorial, authoritarian and non-consultative, non-listening managerial approach; unfair, inconsiderate, inconsistent, and/or self-serving behavior; active intimidating, and/or undermining behavior; slack management, procrastination in decision making, ignoring problems and/or avoiding or abdicating from responsibilities; depriving and/or withholding behavior; exhibits parochial behavior, a closed mind, and/or a negative approach" (p. 7). Hamlin and colleagues derived these behaviors directly from subordinates who were asked to describe ineffective behaviors. These ineffective leaders need to be recognized and trained to be effective leaders, or they get worse and will become toxic, destructive leaders and abusive supervisors.

According to Reed (1994), sub-toxic leaders are "mistrustful and have a situation-based relationship with the truth. They are also insulting and do not give any praise or credit to their subordinates. They attempt to dominate meetings and to destroy teams. They are hypercritical of their peers. They misuse power and make ill-considered decisions" (p. 259).

Ineffective leaders can also be workplace bullies. Workplace bullying creates a toxic environment that impedes the learning and development of employees (Reio Jr. & Ghosh, 2009). Bullying involves a clear intention to hurt the target (Hershcovis, 2011). When a subordinate is repeatedly subjected to negative acts by their supervisor, they are being bullied (Einarsen, 2000).

Hershcovis et al. (2015) notes the following examples of bullying behaviors:

"Taking away responsibility from someone or replacing it with more unpleasant tasks • Ignoring someone's opinions • Persistently criticizing someone's work • Spreading gossip or rumors about someone • Ignoring or excluding someone at work • Hinting to someone that they should quit their job" (p. 4).

Workplace bullying has been researched as a concept with many aspects and features of behavior (Escartín et al., 2010). It is differentiated from other types of aggression by a perpetrator toward a target by the way they systematically, persistently, and negatively act over time (Nielsen et al., 2015). It has also been researched as a way to discriminate (Fevre et al., 2012, 2013) and as a gendered concept (Salin & Hoel, 2013). S is the same as bullying, the only difference is that it occurs online rather than off (Farley et al., 2018). Baruch (2005) found in a study of a large multi-national corporation that managers were more likely than other employees to engage in email cyberbullying toward their direct reports, with employees reporting such behaviors as intimidation and work insults—and even personal threats, by their direct supervisor.

Prevalence

Workplace bullying affects almost 80 million workers in the U.S. (WBI, 2021). Other estimates are 15–50% of workers are affected by bullies (Porter et al., 2018). Nielsen et al. (2010) found 26% of workers in North America were bullied. 65% of bullying is done by supervisors

(WBI, 2021). Namie and Namie (2000) found an even larger percentage (89%) of bullying done by leaders. 72% of workplace bullies were supervisors who abused subordinates, according to a Zogby survey from 2007 (Sutton, 2012).

OUTCOMES

Bullied employees experience anxiety and depression (Hauge et al., 2010; Hansen et al., 2006), as well as anger (Aquino & Lamertz, 2004) and other negative emotions (Bowling & Beehr, 2006; Vie et al., 2012). Victims of bullying also are emotionally exhausted and burnt out (Wu & Hu, 2009).

Porter et al. (2018) report that bullying direct and indirect costs are over $40 billion annually to U.S. organizations. Absenteeism increases (e.g., Kivimäki et al., 2000) along with CWB (Hershcovis et al., 2012) and intention to turnover (Bowling & Beehr 2006; Hershcovis & Barling, 2010). Workplace bullying leads to lower OCB and performance (Harris, 2011; Schat & Frone, 2011; Zellars et al., 2002), less creativity (Mathisen et al., 2008), lower job and life satisfaction, and organizational commitment (Bowling & Beehr, 2006; Hershcovis & Barling, 2010). Valentine et al. (2021) found that workplace bullying also leads to viewing jobs politically and to not trusting others, which in turn leads to less effective work groups and organizations.

GENDER AND INEFFECTIVE LEADERSHIP AND WORKPLACE BULLYING

Women are more likely than men to be the targets of workplace bullying and only 33% of workplace bullies are women (WBI, 2021). Since more men than women are bullies and more women than men are the targets of bullies, most studies research women as the targets of bullies. When women are the bullies, other women are usually the targets (Gardner et al., 2020). Women are less likely to be bullies because they feel it is costlier to them (Rutter & Hine, 2005) due to socialization (McCormack et al., 2018).

CULTURE AND INEFFECTIVE LEADERSHIP
AND WORKPLACE BULLYING

Hamlin et al. (2012) have found that ineffective behaviors have been described in essentially the same way in China, Germany, Canada, Mexico, the U.K. Romania, and Egypt, arguing for the universality of the concept. Ten years later, Patel et al. (2022) reached the same conclusion, that Hofstede's (1991) dimensions do not seem to matter when it comes to employee perceptions of leader behavior, after considering studies in the U.K., Hungary, the Netherlands, the U.A.E., Portugal, France, India, South Korea, India, and Germany.

Toxic behaviors such as workplace bullying are a frequent problem globally. Beghini et al. (2022) found in a global survey that psychological violence and harassment (which included threats, bullying, intimidation, and insults) was the most common form of harassment and violence reported by both genders, with almost 18% or 583 million employees experiencing it at work. Another study found a prevalence of 9.7% in Scandinavia, 15.7% in other European countries, and 26% in North America of employees experiencing bullying (Nielsen et al., 2010). In study in New Zealand, 15% of the participants had experienced bullying, with women reporting more than men.

Employees from cultures with high power distance, such as in Asia, tend to be more accepting of workplace bullying behavior than employees from cultures with lower power distances (Escartín et al., 2011; Loh et al., 2010, 2021). There also may be variance across cultures due to differing definitions of what constitutes bullying behavior (Hershcovis et al., 2015).

CONCLUSION

Ineffective supervisors often also bully their subordinates. Part of their ineffectiveness as supervisors is their poor relationship with their subordinates. While their behavior stops short of the abusiveness of abusive supervisors and destructive leaders, there is still an intent to harm their subordinates, or at least a lack of care and consideration as to whether harm has been done. At the next level on the spectrum is the uncivil leader, whose behavior is ambiguous in terms of whether there is an attempt to harm their subordinate, or whether they are merely rude to everyone.

REFERENCES

Aquino, K. & Lamertz, K. (2004). A relational model of workplace victimization: Social roles and patterns of victimization in dyadic relationships. *Journal of Applied Psychology, 89*, 1023–1034.

Baron-Cohen, S. (2011). *The science of evil: On empathy and the origins of cruelty.* Basic Books.

Baruch, Y. (2005). Bullying on the net: Adverse behavior on e-mail and its impact. *Information & Management, 42*(2), 361–371.

Beghini, V., Cattaneo, U., Dugan, A., & Pozzan, E. (2022). *Experiences of violence and harassment at work: A global first survey.* International Labor Organization. https://webapps.ilo.org/wcmsp5/groups/public/---dgreports/---dcomm/documents/publication/wcms_863095.pdf. Accessed 30 April 2024.

Bowling, N. A., & Beehr, T. A. (2006). Workplace harassment from the victim's perspective: a theoretical model and meta-analysis. *Journal of Applied Psychology, 91*(5), 998.

Douglas, S. C., & Martinko, M. J. (2001). Exploring the role of individual differences in the prediction of workplace aggression. *Journal of Applied Psychology, 86*, 547–559.

Einarsen, S. (2000). Harassment and bullying at work: A review of the Scandinavian approach. *Aggression and Violent Behavior, 5*(4), 379–401.

Escartín, J., Rodríguez-Carballeira, Á., Gómez-Benito, J., & Zapf, D. (2010). Development and validation of the workplace bullying scale EAPA-T. *International Journal of Clinical Health & Psychology, 10*, 519–539.

Escartín, J., Zapf, D., Arrieta, C., & Rodriguez-Carballeira, A. (2011). Workers' perception of workplace bullying: A cross-cultural study. *European Journal of Work and Organizational Psychology*, 1–23. https://doi.org/10.1080/135 94320903395652

Farley, S., Coyne, I., & D'Cruz, P. (2018). Cyberbullying at work: Understanding the influence of technology. In P. D'Cruz, E. Noronha, G. Notelaers, & C. Rayner (Eds.), *Concepts, approaches and methods* (pp. 233–263). Springer. https://doi.org/10.1007/978-981-10-5334-4_8-1

Ferris, D. L., Spence, J. R., Brown, D. J., & Heller, D. (2012). Interpersonal injustice and workplace deviance: The role of esteem threat. *Journal of Management, 38*, 1788–1811.

Ferris, D. L., Rosen, C. C., Johnson, R. E., Brown, D. J., Risavy, S., & Heller, D. (2011). Approach or avoidance (or both?): Integrating core self-evaluations within an approach/avoidance framework. *Personnel Psychology, 64*, 137–161.

Fevre, R., Lewis, D., Robinson, A., & Jones, T. (2012). *Trouble at work.* Bloomsbury.

Fevre, R., Robinson, A., Lewis, D., & Jones, T. (2013). The ill-treatment of employees with disabilities in British workplaces. *Work, Employment and Society, 27*(2), 288–307.

Fox, S., & Spector, P. E. (1999). A model of work frustration–aggression. *Journal of Organizational Behavior, 20*, 915–931.

Gardner, D., Roche, M., Bentley, T., Cooper-Thomas, H., Catley, B., Teo, S., & Trenberth, L. (2020). An exploration of gender and workplace bullying in New Zealand. *International Journal of Manpower, 41*(8), 1385–1395. https://doi.org/10.1108/IJM-02-2019-0067

Hamlin, R. G., Patel, T., Ruiz, C., & Whitford, S. (2012). Towards a universal taxonomy of perceived managerial and leadership effectiveness: A multiple cross-case/cross-nation study of effective and ineffective managerial behaviour. In *Proceedings of the 13th UFHRD International Conference of Human Resource Development Research and Practice across Europe*. UFHRD.

Hansen, Å. M., Hogh, A., Persson, R., Karlson, B., Garde, A. H., & Ørbæk, P. (2006). Bullying at work, health outcomes, and physiological stress response. *Journal of Psychosomatic Research, 60*(1), 63–72.

Harris, M. A. (2011). Personality and Self-Compassion of Former Victims of Bullying. Doctoral Dissertation University of Arizona.

Hauge, L. J., Skogstad, A., & Einarsen, S. (2009). Individual and situational predictors of workplace bullying: Why do perpetrators engage in the bullying of others?. *Work & Stress, 23*(4), 349–358.

Hauge, L. J., Skogstad, A., & Einarsen, S. (2010). The relative impact of workplace bullying as a social stressor at work. *Scandinavian journal of psychology, 51*(5), 426–433.

Hershcovis, M. S. (2011). "Incivility, social undermining, bullying... oh my!": A call to reconcile constructs within workplace aggression research. *Journal of Organizational Behavior, 32*(3), 499–519. https://doi.org/10.1002/job.689

Hershcovis, M. S., Reich, T. C., & Niven, K. (2015). *Workplace bullying: Causes, consequences, and intervention strategies* (SIOP White Paper Series). Society for Industrial and Organizational Psychology.

Hershcovis, M. S., Turner, N., Barling, J., Arnold, K. A., Dupré, K. E., & Sivanathan, N. (2007). Predicting workplace aggression: A meta-analysis. *Journal of Applied Psychology, 92*, 228–238.

Hershcovis, M. S., & Barling, J. (2010). Towards a multi-foci approach to workplace aggression: A meta-analytic review of outcomes from different perpetrators. *Journal of organizational Behavior, 31*(1), 24–44.

Hershcovis, M. S., Reich, T. C., Parker, S. K., & Bozeman, J. (2012). The relationship between workplace aggression and target deviant behaviour: The moderating roles of power and task interdependence. *Work & Stress, 26*(1), 1–20.

Hofstede, G. (1991). Cultures and organizations: Software of the mind. McGraw-Hill.

Keashly, L. (2012). Workplace bullying and gender: It's complicated. In S. Fox & T. R. Lituchy (Eds.), *Gender and the dysfunctional workplace* (pp. 78–95). Edward Elgar.

Kivimäki, M., Elovainio, M., & Vahtera, J. (2000). Workplace bullying and sickness absence in hospital staff. *Occupational and Environmental medicine, 57*(10), 656–660.

Loh, J., Restubog, S. L. D., & Zagenczyk, T. J. (2010). Consequences of workplace bullying on employee identification and satisfaction among Australians and Singaporeans. *Journal of Cross-Cultural Psychology, 41*(2), 236–252. https://doi.org/10.1177/0022022109354641

Loh, J. M., Thorsteinsson, E. B., & Loi, N. M. (2021). Workplace incivility and work outcomes: Cross-cultural comparison between Australian and Singaporean employees. *Asia Pacific Journal of Human Resources, 59*(2), 305–329. https://doi.org/10.1111/1744-7941.12233

Mathisen, G. E., Einarsen, S., & Mykletun, R. (2008). The occurrences and correlates of bullying and harassment in the restaurant sector. *Scandinavian Journal of Psychology, 49*(1), 59–68.

McCormack, D., Djurkovic, N., Nsubuga-Kyobe, A., & Casimir, G. (2018). Workplace bullying: The interactive effects of the perpetrator's gender and the target's gender. *Employee Relations, 40*(2), 264–280.

Namie, G., & Namie, R. (2000). *The bully at work: What you can do to stop the hurt and reclaim the dignity on the job.* Sourcebooks.

Nielsen, M. B., Matthiesen, S. B., & Einarsen, S. (2010). The impact of methodological moderators on prevalence rates of workplace bullying. A meta-analysis. *Journal of Occupational and Organizational Psychology, 83,* 955–979.

Nielsen, M. B., Hoel, H., Zapf, D., & Einarsen, S. (2015). Exposure to aggression in the workplace. In S. Clarke, T. M. Probst, F. Guldenmund, & J. Passmore (Eds.), *The Wiley Blackwell handbook of the psychology of occupational safety and workplace health* (pp. 205–227). Wiley Blackwell.

Patel, T., Hamlin, R. G., & Louis, D. (2022). Toward a generic framework of negative manager/leader behavior: A comparative study across nations and private sector industries. *European Management Review, 1–17,* https://doi.org/10.1111/emre.12507

Porter, T. H., Day, N., & Meglich, P. (2018). City of discontent? The influence of perceived organizational culture, LMX, and newcomer status on reported bullying in a municipal workplace. *Employee Responsibilities and Rights Journal, 30,* 119–141.

Reed, S. F. (1994). *The toxic executive: A step-by-step guide for turning your boss (or yourself) from noxious to nurturing.* Harper Business.

Reio, T. G., & Ghosh, R. (2009). Antecedents and outcomes of workplace incivility: Implications for human resource development research and practice. *Human Resource Development Quarterly, 20*(3), 237–264. https://doi.org/10.1002/hrdq.20020

Rutter, A., & Hine, D. (2005). Sex differences in workplace aggression: An investigation of moderation and mediation effects. *Aggressive Behavior, 31*(3), 254–270.

Salin, D., & Hoel, H. (2013). Workplace bullying as a gendered phenomenon. *Journal of Managerial Psychology, 28*(3), 235–251.

Schat, A. C., & Frone, M. R. (2011). Exposure to psychological aggression at work and job performance: The mediating role of job attitudes and personal health. *Work & Stress, 25*(1), 23–40.

Sutton, R. I. (2012). Good boss, bad boss: How to be the best... and learn from the worst. *Business Plus.*

Valentine, S. R., Giacalone, R. A., & Fleischman, G. (2021). Workplace bullying, socially aversive attitudes, reduced work group effectiveness, and organizational frustration. *Human Resource Development Quarterly, 32*(2), 131–153. https://doi.org/10.1002/hrdq.21418

Vie, T. L., Glasø, L., & Einarsen, S. (2012). How does it feel? Workplace bullying, emotions and musculoskeletal complaints. *Scandinavian Journal of Psychology, 53*(2), 165–173.

Workplace Bullying Institute (WBI). (2021). *Results of the 2021 WBI U.S. Workplace Bullying Survey.* https://workplacebullying.org/2021-wbi-survey/. Accessed 8 July 2024.

Zellars, K. L., Tepper, B. J., & Duffy, M. K. (2002). Abusive supervision and subordinates' organizational citizenship behavior. *Journal of Applied Psychology, 87*, 1068–1076. https://doi.org/10.1037/0021-9010.87.6.1068

Wu, T. Y., & Hu, C. (2009). Abusive supervision and employee emotional exhaustion: Dispositional antecedents and boundaries. Group & Organization Management, 34(2), 143–169.

CHAPTER 5

Uncivil Leaders

Abstract This chapter describes uncivil leaders. Incivility is a big problem globally. Unlike bullying, incivility has an ambiguous intent to harm the subordinate. This leader has a moderate amount of empathy. Their empathy circuit temporarily turns off and lets them behave in a hurtful manner toward them. Uncivil leaders are the most common bad leaders on the spectrum. Incivility leads to job dissatisfaction and decreased employee well-being and affective commitment to the organization.

Keywords Uncivil leaders · Incivility

The U.S. is known for its over-active work ethic. Americans are the most overworked globally. Jimmy Buffet sang about bosses watching workers with cameras. Some U.S. companies typify this behavior. According to a recent Oxfam report, Amazon and Walmart are good examples (Oxfam, 2024). 53% of Amazon workers who work in its warehouses feel like they are being monitored or watched almost all of the time. 56% felt anxious or depressed in the last two weeks for at least several days. Amazon tracks its workers to increase its productivity. And the monitoring is constant.

Many American bosses are what Reed (1994) calls the tyro-toxic leader. This leader behaves in ways that are mildly abusive to the employee. "They are suspicious and unfriendly, unable to share credit or

B. W. Eversole, *The Leadership Spectrum*,
https://doi.org/10.1007/978-3-031-73557-8_5

give praise, they don't listen to others and don't communicate with their peers. Having a secret agenda, they disrupt meetings and are indecisive" (p. 259).The uncivil leader would be at level 3 empathy (Baron-Cohen, 2011). They have difficulty with empathy and social interaction. They have a tough time reading their employees' faces and are never sure what is expected of them. This is the level on the continuum where leaders start moving toward the dark triad.

Defined

Tyro-toxic leaders are also uncivil. Uncivil behavior is to behave in a rude, impolite, and discourteous manner (Alola & Alola, 2018). Andersson and Pearson (1999) defined incivility as "low intensity deviant behavior with ambiguous intent to harm the target, in violation of workplace norms for mutual respect. Uncivil behaviors are characteristically rude, discourteous, displaying a lack of respect for others"(p. 457). Welbourne et al. (2020) defined incivility as "low intensity negative behaviors that violate workplace norms of respect" (p. 335).

Behavior

Examples of uncivil behavior include ignoring calls and messages and side talk (Pearson et al., 2001), ignoring a colleague's ideas or excluding them from an important meeting, or talking with them unprofessionally (Welbourne et al., 2020). Ghosh et al. (2013) found the following supervisor incivility behaviors: "Put you down or was condescending to you; paid little attention to your statements or showed little interest in your opinion; made demeaning or derogatory remarks about you; addressed you in unprofessional terms, either publicly or privately; ignored or excluded you from professional camaraderie; doubted your judgment on a matter over which you have responsibility; made unwanted attempts to draw you into a discussion of personal matters; gave you the silent treatment; did not give you credit where credit was due; talked about you behind your back; gave you dirty looks or negative eye contact; and cut you off in the middle of a conversation without regard for your feelings" (p. 179). It is particularly important that these uncivil behaviors by a supervisor need to be recognized and remediated by training and development, or the supervisor will become a sub-toxic, ineffective leader, rather than a civil and effective leader. Moreover, Baron-Cohen (2011) notes that when we start to objectify a person and at the same time, we turn off our sensitivity to their emotions, (our empathy circuit goes down) that starts us down the road to zero degrees of empathy. Empathy erosion is not only an organizational issue, but a global one affecting families, communities, and nations (Baron-Cohen, 2011). And it starts when we become uncivil toward each other.

Even judges have been accused of uncivil behavior. A judge was suspended in 2021 after she pushed and yelled at employees, yelling at other judges, and exhibiting "uncontrollable incivility" (Knezevich, 2021). Talking over each other and also over the moderator for a quarter of their debate in 2020, candidates Trump and Biden also engaged in incivility that was considered to be surprising to even viewers who were jaded (Zarracina & Petras, 2020).

Prevalence

Estimates as high as 13–36% of workers report to leaders who are dysfunctional (this percentage would include abusive/destructive and ineffective/bullying leaders as well) (Rose et al., 2015). In a study done by Erickson (2007) of 345 employees in the U.S. and Australia, they found that bad leaders were quite common in their organizations.

Incivility has been experienced by almost everyone (Alola & Alola, 2018). Porath and Pearson (2013) polled employees over 14 years and found that 98% of them experienced incivility at work. 25% said they experienced it weekly in 1998; that doubled to 50% in 2011, and by 2016, it had increased to 62% (Porath, 2022).

A recent survey of over 1000 employees in the U.S. by the Society of Human Resource Management (Gonzales, 2024) found that 66% either experienced incivility themselves or witnessed it within the past month, while 57% either experienced it or witnessed it within the past week. Frontline employees may be experiencing incivility at a greater rate than general employees. Supervisors frequently behave in an uncivil manner toward their direct reports (Johnson & Indvik, 2001; Porath & Pearson, 2012). Reio Jr. and Ghosh (2009) reported that 54% of respondents admitted to instigating uncivil behaviors in the workplace, such as saying something hurtful or making fun of someone, at least once a year. Top-down workplace incivility is 60% of workplace incivility (Sutton, 2012).

OUTCOMES

Workplace incivility is clearly on the rise and is unhealthy for both the organization and its employees (Porath & Pearson, 2013), affecting their well-being in a negative way (Cortina et al., 2001). Incivility is especially stressful after many occurrences resulting in an adverse outcome (Andersson & Pearson, 1999). Research by scholars (Cortina et al., 2001; Lim & Cortina, 2005; Tremmel & Sonnentag, 2018) suggest that the experience of incivility leads employees to be dissatisfied with their jobs, experience decreased physical and psychological well-being, and have decreased affective commitment to their jobs. Targets of incivility are also exhausted (Rhee et al., 2017; van Jaarsveld et al., 2010). Victims of incivility are more likely to engage in CWB (Welbourne & Sariol, 2017) and incivility themselves toward their colleagues (Gallus et al., 2014).

Stress from incivility arises from negative emotions which affect employee well-being (Bunk & Magley, 2013; Lim et al., 2008). Lim et al. (2018) noted that the stress from incivility occurs both over the long term due to repeated uncivil incidents, but also during the day when the uncivil incident occurs. Incivility is also associated with depression (Miner et al., 2012) and burnout (Miner-Rubino & Reed, 2010).

Ghosh et al. (2013) noted that supervisor incivility had both a direct and indirect effect on turnover intention. Alola and Alola (2018) studied the effect of resilience on workplace incivility and intention to turnover. They found that resilience mediated the relationship, but also found that workplace incivility had a detrimental effect on employees. Direct reports rarely retaliate against their supervisors, fearing counterretaliation and punishment due to the power-differential (Aquino et al., 2001).

So, what is the role of trust in the relationship between employee and the uncivil supervisor? Saleem et al.'s (2022) study seems to suggest that employees can overlook the uncivil behavior of a supervisor if they trust them. However, Jawahar and Schreurs (2018)'s research showed if an employee trusts their supervisor, it actually makes the incivility from the supervisor even worse because it violates the expectations of a trusting relationship. If the employee does not trust their supervisor, then the incivility doesn't matter that much because the employee did not have many expectations anyway. According to Rawat et al. (2020) "one of the fallouts of the absence of trust is the rise of workplace incivility" (p. 302).

Porath and Gerbasi (2015) found that uncivil employees don't necessarily mean to be uncivil; only four percent stated that they are uncivil because they can get away with it and it is fun. Generally, uncivil behavior occurs because the person doesn't understand their effect on the other person; they do not understand how they are perceived. This means that uncivil leaders should be ready to be trained to be civil, once they understand the effect that they have on others and how they are being perceived when they exhibit uncivil behaviors. Once the unconscious incompetence is made conscious, then change can occur (Broadwell, 1969). Empathy training can also help to increase their empathy.

GENDER AND INCIVILITY

Men are more likely than women to be the instigators of incivility (Cortina et al., 2001; Gallus et al., 2014; Pearson & Porath, 2005; Pearson et al., 2000), while women are more likely to be the target (Smith et al., 2021). Men are more likely to be rude when the target has low power in the organization, while women are just as likely to be uncivil to those who are in power as those who are not (Pearson et al., 2000). Men seem to be more influenced by situational and environmental and social cues than women (Gallus et al., 2014).

CULTURE AND INCIVILITY

Most incivility research has been done in Western contexts, with only a few studies done in Eastern cultures (Loh et al., 2021). When working in multi-cultural environments, leaders may be unintentionally uncivil because they do not understand the culture and how they will affect others (Porath & Gerbasi, 2015). Loh et al. (2021) similarly found that culture needs to be taken into account with incivility. For example, power distance or individualistic/collectivist cultures (Hofstede, 2001) may result in differences in what is considered rude or uncivil behavior. Moreover, in cultures with high power distance, subordinates tend to be more accepting of supervisors who mistreat them (Lian et al. 2012; Loh et al., 2021). In 2022, Porath conducted a new global survey of more than 2000 frontline employees in over 25 industries and those who observed them. She found that 76% of them experienced incivility at least once a month; 78% observed incivility at work at least once a month with 70% observing it 2–3 times a month.

Conclusion

Uncivil leaders are the final bad leaders on the leadership spectrum. Most bad leaders fall in this category. A large amount of literature exists on incivility, as it is not only leaders who can be uncivil. However, we are focused on the uncivil leader's relationship with their direct reports, which is an ambiguous intent to harm them. We now turn to considering good, or positive, leaders. If uncivil leaders are the most common bad leader, then civil leaders are the most common good leader, doing the bare minimum to be a good supervisor.

References

Alola, U. V., & Alola, A. A. (2018). Can resilience help? Coping with job stressor. *Academic Journal of Economic Studies, 4*(1), 141–152.

Andersson, L. M., & Pearson, C. M. (1999). Tit for tat? The spiraling effect of incivility in the workplace. *Academy of Management Review, 24*, 452–471.

Aquino, K., Tripp, T. M., & Bies, R. J. (2001). How employees respond to personal offense: The effects of blame attribution, victim status, and offender status on revenge and reconciliation in the workplace. *Journal of Applied Psychology, 86*, 52–59.

Baron-Cohen, S. (2011). *The science of evil: On empathy and the origins of cruelty.* Basic Books.

Broadwell, M. M. (1969). Teaching for Learning. *The Gospel Guardian, 20*(41), 1–3.

Bunk, J. A., & Magley, V. J. (2013). The role of appraisals and emotions in understanding experiences of workplace incivility. *Journal of Occupational Health Psychology, 18*(1), 87–105. https://doi.org/10.1037/a0030987

Cortina, L. M., Magley, V. J., Williams, J. H., & Langhout, R. D. (2001). Incivility in the workplace. *Journal of Occupational Health Psychology, 6*(1), 64–80.

Gallus, J. A., Bunk, J. A., Matthews, R. A., Barnes-Farrell, J. L., & Magley, V. J. (2014). An eye for an eye? Exploring the relationship between workplace incivility experiences and perpetration. *Journal of Occupational Health Psychology, 19*(2), 143–154. https://doi.org/10.1037/a0035931

Ghosh, R., Reio, T. G., & Bang, H. (2013). Reducing turnover intent: Supervisor and co-worker incivility and socialization-related learning. *Human Resource Development International, 16*(2), 169–185. https://doi.org/10.1080/13678868.2012.756199

Gonzales, M. (2024, March 6). Workplace incivility is more common than you think. https://www.shrm.org/topics-tools/news/inclusion-equity-diversity/workplace-incivility-shrm-research-2024#:~:text=The%20survey%20of%20over%201%2C000,work%20within%20the%20past%20week. Accessed 24 April 2024.

Hofstede, G. (2001). *Culture's consequences: Comparing values, behaviors, institutions and organizations across nations* (2nd ed.). Sage.

Jawahar, I. M., & Schreurs, B. (2018). Supervisor incivility and how it affects subordinates' performance: A matter of trust. *Personnel Review, 47*(3), 709–726.

Johnson, P. R., & Indvik, J. (2001). Slings and arrows of rudeness: Incivility in the workplace. *Journal of Management Development, 20*(8), 705–714.

Knezevich, A. (2021, July 1). 'Uncontrollable incivility:' Baltimore judge suspended without pay by Maryland Court of Appeals. *The Baltimore Sun*.

Lim, S., & Cortina, L. M. (2005). Interpersonal mistreatment in the workplace: The interface and impact of general incivility and sexual harassment. *Journal of Applied Psychology, 90*, 483–496.

Lim, S., Cortina, L. M., & Magley, V. J. (2008). Personal and workgroup incivility: Impact on work and health outcomes. *Journal of Applied Psychology, 93*(1), 95–107. https://doi.org/10.1037/0021-9010.93.1.95

Lim, S., Ilies, R., Koopman, J., Christoforou, P., & Arvey, R. D. (2018). Emotional mechanisms linking incivility at work to aggression and withdrawal at home: An experience-sampling study. *Journal of Management, 44*(7), 2888–2908.

Loh, J. M., Thorsteinsson, E. B., & Loi, N. M. (2021). Workplace incivility and work outcomes: Cross-cultural comparison between Australian and Singaporean employees. *Asia Pacific Journal of Human Resources, 59*(2), 305–329. https://doi.org/10.1111/1744-7941.12233

Lian, H., Ferris, D. L., & Brown, D. J. (2012). Does power distance exacerbate or mitigate the effects of abusive supervision? It depends on the outcome. *Journal of Applied Psychology, 97*(1), 107–123. https://doi.org/10.1037/a0024610

Miner-Rubino, K., & Reed, W. D. (2010). Testing a moderated mediational model of workgroup incivility: The roles of organizational trust and group regard. *Journal of Applied Social Psychology, 40*(12), 3148–3168.

Miner, K. N., Settles, I. H., Pratt-Hyatt, J. S., & Brady, C. C. (2012). Experiencing incivility in organizations: The buffering effects of emotional and organizational support. *Journal of Applied Social Psychology, 42*(2), 340–372.

Oxfam. (2024, April 10). Is Amazon a good place to work? https://www.oxfamamerica.org/explore/stories/is-amazon-a-good-place-to-work/. Accessed 29 July 2024.

Pearson, C. M., Andersson, L. M., & Porath, C. L. (2000). Assessing and attacking workplace incivility. *Organizational Dynamics, 29*, 123–137.

Pearson, C. M., Andersson, L. M., & Wegner, J. W. (2001). When workers flout convention: A study of workplace incivility. *Human Relations, 54*(11), 1387–1419.

Pearson, C. M., & Porath, C. L. (2005). On the nature, consequences and remedies of workplace incivility: No time for "nice"? Think Again. *Academy of Management Perspectives, 19*(1), 7–18.

Porath, C. (2022, November 9). Frontline work when everyone is angry. https://hbr.org/2022/11/frontline-work-when-everyone-is-angry Accessed 24 April 2024.

Porath, C. L., & Gerbasi, A. (2015). Does civility pay? *Organizational Dynamics, 44*(4), 281–286. https://doi.org/10.1016/j.orgdyn.2015.09.005

Porath, C. L., & Pearson, C. M. (2012). Emotional and behavioral responses to workplace incivility and the impact of hierarchical status. *Journal of Applied Social Psychology, 42*(S1), E326–E357. https://doi.org/10.1111/j.1559-1816.2012.01020.x

Porath, C., & Pearson, C. (2013). The price of incivility. *Harvard Business Review, 91*(1–2), 114–121.

Rawat, P. S., Bhattacharjee, S. B., & Ganesh, V. (2020). Selective incivility, trust and general well-being: A study of women at workplace. *Journal of Indian Business Research, 12*(3), 303–326.

Reed, S. F. (1994). *The toxic executive: A step-by-step guide for turning your boss (or yourself) from noxious to nurturing.* Harper Business.

Reio, T. G., & Ghosh, R. (2009). Antecedents and outcomes of workplace incivility: Implications for human resource development research and practice. *Human Resource Development Quarterly, 20*(3), 237–264. https://doi.org/10.1002/hrdq.20020

Rhee, S.-Y., Hur, W.-M., & Kim, M. (2017). The relationship of coworker incivility to job performance and the moderating role of self-efficacy and compassion at work: The job demands-resources (JD-R) approach. *Journal of Business and Psychology, 32*, 711–726. https://doi.org/10.1007/s10869-016-9469-2

Rose, K., Shuck, B., Twyford, D., & Bergman, M. (2015). Skunked: An integrative review exploring the consequences of the dysfunctional leader and implications for those employees who work for them. *Human Resource Development Review, 14*(1), 64–90.

Saleem, F., Malik, M. I., Asif, I., & Qasim, A. (2022). Workplace incivility and employee performance: Does trust in supervisors matter? (A dual theory perspective). *Behavioral Sciences, 12*(12), 513. https://doi.org/10.3390/bs1212050513

Smith, A. E., Hassan, S., Hatmaker, D. M., DeHart-Davis, L., & Humphrey, N. (2021). Gender, race, and experiences of workplace incivility in public organizations. *Review of Public Personnel Administration, 41*(4), 674–699.

Sutton, R. I. (2012). *Good boss, bad boss: How to be the best... and learn from the worst.* Business Plus.

Tremmel, S., & Sonnentag, S. (2018). A sorrow halved? A daily diary study on talking about experienced workplace incivility and next morning negative affect. *Journal of Occupational Health Psychology, 23*, 568–583. https://doi.org/10.1037/ocp0000100

van Jaarsveld, D. D., Walker, D. D., & Skarlicki, D. P. (2010). The role of job demands and emotional exhaustion in the relationship between customer and employee incivility. *Journal of Management, 36*, 1486–1504. https://doi.org/10.1177/0149206310368998

Welbourne, J. L., Miranda, G., & Gangadharan, A. (2020). Effects of employee personality on the relationships between experienced incivility, emotional exhaustion, and perpetrated incivility. *International Journal of Stress Management, 27*(4), 335–345. https://doi.org/10.1037/str0000160

Welbourne, J. L., & Sariol, A. M. (2017). When does incivility lead to counterproductive work behavior? Roles of job involvement, task interdependence, and gender. *Journal of Occupational Health Psychology, 22*(2), 194–206. https://doi.org/10.1037/ocp0000029

Zarracina, J., & Petras, P. (2020, Oct. 1). Trump, Biden debate was exchange of insults and incivility. See for yourself. *USA Today.* https://usatoday.com/in-depth/news/2020/10/01/2020-debate-trump-biden-presidential-debate-campaign/5879363002/. Accessed 24 April 2024.

Positive Leaders

CHAPTER 6

Civil Transactional Leader

Abstract This chapter describes the first positive leader in the spectrum. This leader is civil, rather than uncivil. They lead in a respectful way within work norms, using a transactional leadership style. This leader has an average amount of empathy for their direct reports and does not wish to harm them. They can be trained to be effective leaders. Civil leaders use a transactional leadership style. Civility increases work engagement and decreases turnover.

Keywords Civil leader · Civility · Transactional leader · Transactional leadership

CIVILITY

Civil leaders do the bare minimum to be a good supervisor. These leaders would be at level 4 of empathy (Baron-Cohen, 2011), so these leaders don't really like talking about feelings. At level 4, managers prefer technical problems to having discussions about emotions (Baron-Cohen, 2011).

Defined

The civil leader is one who behaves within work norms, with good manners, and is respectful to others (Andersson & Pearson, 1999). Civility can be thought of as a moral basis for all relationships between people building on respect (Carter, 1998) or simply being considerate of other people in relationships (Ferriss, 2002). To be civil is to be able to exercise restraint and self-discipline, especially to be in control of one's anger, and to be able to let go of behaviors that inflate one's ego (Ferriss, 2002).

Behaviors

Civil leaders do the opposite of what uncivil leaders do. Civil leaders do not raise their voice, they do not criticize their employees in front of others, they give feedback at least once a year at the performance appraisal review, they catch their employees doing something right once in a while. They do not do anything that is abusive, yet they do not try to find out what is motivating to the employee, and they do not attempt to coach the employee to improve their performance either. They are not condescending, they pay attention to their employees and are interested in their opinions; they do not make demeaning or derogatory remarks about their employees; they always address them professionally; they do not doubt their judgment on matters over which they have responsibility; they do not make unwanted attempts to draw them into discussion of personal matters; they never give their employees the silent treatment; they give their employees credit when credit is due; they never talk about their employees behind their back; they don't give their employees dirty looks; and they don't cut their subordinates off in the middle of a conversation. This leader can be trained and developed to be an effective leader.

Outcomes

When subordinates feel respected by their supervisor, they are more likely to be committed to interacting and participating with them (Gill & Sypher, 2010). Civil behaviors like respect influence the trust that a subordinate has in their leader (Laschinger & Finegan, 2005). Being respected and appreciated by supervisors creates a civil workplace and reduces incivility (Wiesenfeld et al., 2001). In fact, civility predicts turnover

(Laschinger et al., 2009; Yanchus et al., 2017), as does the relationship with one's supervisor (Rhoades & Eisenberger, 2002) and unhappiness at work (Collini et al., 2015). As we noted in the Introduction, people leave bosses, not organizations. Yet bosses can create uncivil organizations that make people want to leave.

Compared to research on incivility, research on workplace civility is comparatively scant, despite studies showing that civil workplaces have benefits such as better mental and physical well-being for employees, lower absenteeism, and lower burnout (Peng, 2023). Sadaqat et al. (2022) noted that managers should provide support and be fair to their direct reports to make sure that their organizations have a healthy environment in order to promote civility. Civil leaders improve the motivation and work engagement of their subordinates (Alam et al., 2021).

Tate and White (2005) note that David Berlo (p. 18) used the phrase "I mean you no harm," when describing the work environment that managers should create for their employees in order to ensure high performance levels. This environment should be one where direct reports are treated fairly, with dignity and respect, are trusted, with equity and sincerity. Fear, intimidation, and stress are not present in the work environment. Without this basis, supervisors cannot expect motivation or a desire for performance; in other words, this is the bare minimum that supervisors should provide for their direct reports in their relationship with them. Anderson (2022) notes that knowing your people is the bare minimum. Ask them every week how things are going, what help they need from you, and to give you any feedback about what is going on. Be sure to listen to them and show gratitude that they have shared this with you.

Maslow's (1970) hierarchy of needs explains the bare minimum that employees need to be satisfied at work. They need to have the lower levels met before the higher levels. Physiological needs are the first level, followed by safety, belonging and love, self-esteem, and then self-actualization. Kahn (2010) noted that a leader should create a work environment where as many of these needs are met as possible. According to Shuck and Herd (2012), Maslow applies to the motivation of direct reports of a leader in that they are motivated by fulfilling their unsatisfied needs at their lowest level.

Most people want a boss who is trusting, builds rapport and is considerate (Babiak & Hare, 2019). Most relationships are built upon trust and trust affects all levels of human relationships (Mayer & Gavin, 2005).

Trust can be defined as the willingness of someone to be vulnerable to what another person does (Mayer et al., 1995). Trust not only is the foundation of an advantageous work environment between a leader and their direct report (Jawahar & Schreurs, 2018), but Chughtai et al. (2015) found that trusting one's leader is associated with work engagement. Dirks and Ferrin (2002) and Colquitt et al. (2007) each found a positive relationship between trust in one's supervisor and employee performance. Empathy is important in developing trust between a leader and their direct reports (Rahman, 2016). Leaders need to be open and transparent with them in order to build trust (Martinovski et al., 2007; Tager, 2004).

Rawat et al. (2020) showed that especially for women, trust in one's supervisor led to civil behavior. Rawat et al. (2020) also showed that increased civility occurs when there is trust between leaders and their direct reports, and that this has a positive relationship with employee well-being. Studies show that civility in the workplace can also reduce turnover (Ismail et al., 2018; Pearson & Porath, 2005).

Trust is even more important today in the days of remote and hybrid working. As Sokolic (2022) noted "research on the future of work consistently predicts that remote working, and especially working from home, will become as widespread as the more traditional alternative of working on the employer's premises" (p. 209). Supervisors find it more difficult to trust remote employees (Mat-Artun & Küskü, 2024; Oldham, 2022; Parker et al., 2020; cf Schuster, 2024). Part of this lack of trust could be due to the inability to directly observe remote subordinates. Gong et al. (2023) offer several suggestions for how supervisors can become more knowledgeable about the accomplishments of their remote workers. Competent communication is also a component of trustworthiness of supervisors (Mikkelson et al., 2021) and effective communication predicted empowerment, engagement, and accomplishment of both remote and hybrid employees (Mikkelson et al., 2024). The same study found that appropriate communication predicted less stress, burnout, and turnover. Similarly, Adnams (2020) noted the need for effective communication and "understanding the mindset" of the remote and hybrid workforce. Creating opportunities for social exchanges and extra communication opportunities will also help supervisors build trust with remote and hybrid employees (Sarkisian, 2022; Sokolic, 2022). Supervisors need to learn to "check in" with rather than "check-up" on remote workers (Parker et al., 2020). Pennanen (2022) found in their study that in addition to trust, empathy, and understanding were also important in supervising hybrid employees. Parker et al. (2020) also found that supervisors who had low trust in their remote employees also had supervisors who had low trust in them.

Transactional Leadership

Civil leaders practice transactional leadership.

Defined

Transactional leadership is a leadership style centered on trading assets (Bass, 1985). There are three behavioral dimensions: management by exception, both active and passive, and contingent reward (Rockstuhl et al., 2023). Active management by exception means the leader is proactive about surfacing problems before they happen and taking corrective action; passive management means waiting until the problem occurs first.

Behaviors

Transactional leaders utilize praise, rewards and punishments in exchange with their subordinates so that they will achieve goals and objectives using the performance appraisal process (Bass, 1985). However, subordinates will only be motivated to achieve expectations set by the leader (Bass, 1999). Utilizing feedback and goal and role clarity, transactional leaders motivate subordinates to meet their goals (Bass et al., 2003; Politis, 2002). They provide resources and set targets along with providing incentives in exchange for performance, productivity, and task completion (Potosky & Azan, 2023; Wang et al., 2011). However, they also utilize power in order to make sure that necessary tasks are performed (Leitão et al., 2023).

Transactional leadership is composed of two behaviors: active management by exception and contingent reward (Bass, 1999; Eagly et al., 2003). Using contingent rewards will help transactional leaders to influence their subordinates' engagement and autonomy on a daily basis and reward employees for meeting goals (Breevaart et al., 2014; Lai, 2011). Active management by exception (MBE) leaders are always evaluating their employees' performance (Lai, 2011).

Outcomes

There is evidence that using transactional leadership negatively affects the mental health of subordinates (Patrick, 2023). Patrick (2023) found that a focus on rewards can create a harmful competitive culture, making decisions independently can lead to mistrust, and focusing on behavior correction leads to less inclusivity. Moreover, he found that subordinates who were afraid to make mistakes were also worried and anxious, leading to feelings of underappreciation, devaluation, and a lack of job security. Transactional leaders may lack enough empathy when focusing on punishment and correcting behavior, ignoring their subordinates' worried feelings.

A transactional leadership style can also affect the flexibility and creativity of subordinates because of the focus on rule enforcement (Jaqua & Jaqua, 2021). Studies have also shown a negative relationship between transactional leadership and job performance of subordinates (Padmakumar & Dwivedi, 2021; Pedraja-Rejas et al., 2006) as well as on job satisfaction (Kalu, 2010).

GENDER AND CIVIL TRANSACTIONAL LEADERS

Men are more likely to use transactional leadership behaviors than women (Alimo-Metcalfe, 2004; Powell et al., 2004; Rahman et al., 2014). When utilizing transactional leadership behaviors, women were more likely to utilize contingent rewards rather than management by exception, which has been found to be the most effective element of the style (Eagly et al., 2003; Gartzia & van Engen, 2012).

CULTURE AND CIVIL TRANSACTIONAL LEADERS

Civil leaders are viewed as warm and competent, and these traits are universally used by people in different cultures to judge whether or not to support, follow, trust, or build relationships with them (Porath & Gerbasi, 2015). Nevertheless, the authors point out that civil behaviors vary by national culture, especially non-verbal behaviors such as gestures and eye contact. They provide an example of a Japanese manager who was asked in a U.S. organization to give direct feedback to their subordinate about their performance. It was very difficult for them to give critical feedback in a way that was understood. Norms about respect from the civil leader can also vary by national culture, so the leader needs to be mindful of what the subordinate expects and how they will feel, based on their national culture (Porath & Gerbasi, 2015).

Bass and Riggio (2005) claimed that transactional leadership behaviors transcend national culture, in agreement with Patel et al. (2022), Hamlin et al. (2012, 2023). Jackson et al. (2013) agreed with this assertion in their meta-analysis. They found that the relationship between contingent reward and management by exception and affective commitment did not differ across national cultures.

Shahin and Wright (2004) tested this assertion in their study in Egypt, a high power distance country (Hofstede, 1991). They surveyed leaders and their direct reports on transactional leadership and had mixed results. Kalu (2010) did a study in Nigeria, another high power distance country, and found that transactional leadership had a low relationship with subordinate job satisfaction. A study by Cho et al. (2019), however, showed that transactional leadership was positively related to affective organizational commitment in their Korean sample (a high power distance country) but not the U.S. (a low power distance country).

CONCLUSION

Being a civil leader improves individual outcomes (Porath et al., 2015; cf Forni, 2002; Judge et al., 2012). Porath et al. (2015) found that civil employees were viewed as not only warm, but also competent, and were looked on as leaders. Civil leaders are able to form connections, establish healthy cultures, bring out the best in their teams, help their people work better together, and are successful and influential (Porath et al., 2015; Stephens et al., 2011). In Porath et al.'s (2015) study, it is probable that these civil leaders were also effective leaders, as we will discuss in the next chapter.

REFERENCES

Adnams, S. (2020). The distributed workplace of the future is now. *Gartner, Report G00726412.*

Alam, M., Fozia, G. U. L., & Imran, M. (2021). The impact of ethical leadership & civility on organizational commitment: The mediating role of work engagement. *Journal of Arts & Social Sciences, 8*(1), 173–188.

Alimo-Metcalfe, B. (2004). Leadership: A masculine past, but a feminine future? In *Gender and Excellence in the Making* (pp. 161–168). European Commission.

Anderson, D. (2022). *A guide to bare minimum management*. https://www.sca rletink.com/p/guide-to-bare-minimum-management. Accessed 7 June 2024.

Andersson, L. M., & Pearson, C. M. (1999). Tit for tat? The spiraling effect of incivility in the workplace. *Academy of Management Review, 24*, 452–471.

Babiak, P., & Hare, R. D. (2019). *Snakes in suits: When psychopaths go to work*. HarperCollins.

Baron-Cohen, S. (2011). *The science of evil: On empathy and the origins of cruelty*. Basic Books.

Bass, B.M. (1985). *Leadership and performance beyond expectation*. The Free Press.

Bass, B. M. (1999). Two decades of research and development in transformational leadership. *European Journal of Work and Organizational Psychology, 8*, 9–32. https://doi.org/10.1080/135943299398410

Bass, B. M., Avolio, B. J., Jung, D. I., & Berson, Y. (2003). Predicting unit performance by assessing transformational and transactional leadership. *Journal of Applied Psychology, 88*(2), 207.

Bass, B. M., & Riggio, R. E. (2005). *Transformational leadership* (2nd ed.). Psychology Press.

Breevaart, K., Bakker, A. B., Hetland, J., Demerouti, E., Olsen, O. K., & Espevik, R. (2014). Daily transactional and transformational leadership and daily employee engagement. *Journal of Occupational and Organizational Psychology, 87*, 138–157. https://doi.org/10.1111/joop.12041

Carter, S. L. (1998). *Civility: Manners, morals, and the etiquette of democracy*. Basic Books.

Cho, Y., Shin, M., Billing, T. K., & Bhagat, R. S. (2019). Transformational leadership, transactional leadership, and affective organizational commitment: A closer look at their relationships in two distinct national contexts. *Asian Business & Management, 18*, 187–210. https://doi.org/10.1057/s41291-019-00059-1

Chughtai, A., Byrne, M., & Flood, B. (2015). Linking ethical leadership to employee well-being: The role of trust in supervisor. *Journal of Business Ethics, 128*, 653–663.

Colquitt, J. A., Scott, B. A., & LePine, J. A. (2007). Trust, trustworthiness, and trust propensity: A meta-analytic test of their unique relationships with risk taking and job performance. *Journal of Applied Psychology, 92*(4), 909.

Collini, S. A., Guidroz, A. M., & Perez, L. M. (2015). Turnover in health care: The mediating effects of employee engagement. *Journal of Nursing Management, 23*(2), 169–178.

Dirks, K. T., & Ferrin, D. L. (2002). Trust in leadership: Meta-analytic findings and implications for research and practice. *Journal of Applied Psychology*, *87*(4), 611.

Eagly, A. H., Johannesen-Schmidt, M. C., & van Engen, M. L. (2003). Transformational, transactional, and laissez-faire leadership styles: A meta-analysis comparing women and men. *Psychological Bulletin*, *129*, 569–591. https://doi.org/10.1037/0033-2909.129.4.569

Ferriss, A. L. (2002). Studying and measuring civility: A framework, trends and scale. *Sociological Inquiry*, *72*(3), 376–392.

Forni, P. M. (2002). *Choosing civility: The twenty-five rules of considerate conduct.* Martin's Press Griffin.

Gartzia, L., & Van Engen, M. (2012). Are (male) leaders "feminine" enough? Gendered traits of identity as mediators of sex differences in leadership styles. *Gender in Management: An International Journal*, *27*(5), 296–314. https://doi.org/10.1108/17542411211252624

Gill, M. J., & Sypher, B. D. (2010). Workplace incivility and organizational trust. In P. Lutgen-Sandvik & B. D. Sypher (Eds.), *Destructive Organizational Communication* (pp. 69–90). Routledge.

Gong, B., Tobias, P., & Young-Bristol, J. (2023). Leveraging resources to improve supervisors' vision in the remote workplace. *Management Research Review*, *46*(6), 777–789. https://doi.org/10.1108/MRR-12-2021-0916

Hofstede, G. (1991). *Cultures and organizations: Software of the mind.* McGraw-Hill.

Hamlin, R. G., Patel, T., Ruiz, C., & Whitford, S. (2012). Towards a universal taxonomy of perceived managerial and leadership effectiveness: A multiple cross-case/cross-nation study of effective and ineffective managerial behaviour. In *Proceedings of the 13th UFHRD International Conference of Human Resource Development Research and Practice across Europe.* UFHRD.

Hamlin, R. G., Ruiz, C. E., Jones, J., & Patel, T. (2023). Toward a universalistic behavioral model of perceived managerial and leadership effectiveness for the health services sector. *Health Services Management Research*, *36*(2), 89–101. https://doi.org/10.1177/09514848211065462

Ismail, I. R., Poon, J. M., & Arshad, R. (2018). Effects of workplace incivility, negative affectivity and hurt feelings on coworker helping. *Jurnal Pengurusan*, *52*(52), 1–21.

Jackson, T. A., Meyer, J. P., & Wang, X. H. (2013). Leadership, commitment, and culture: A meta-analysis. *Journal of Leadership & Organizational Studies*, *20*(1), 84–106.

Jaqua, E., & Jaqua, T. (2021). Transactional leadership. *American Journal of Biomedical Science and Research*, *14*(5), 399–400.

Jawahar, I. M., & Schreurs, B. (2018). Supervisor incivility and how it affects subordinates' performance: A matter of trust. *Personnel Review, 47*(3), 709–726.

Judge, T. A., Livingston, B. A., & Hurst, C. (2012). Do nice guys—And gals—Really finish last? The joint effects of sex and agreeableness on income. *Journal of Personality and Social Psychology, 102*(2), 390. https://doi.org/10.1037/a0026021

Kahn, W. (2010). The essence of employee engagement: Lessons from the field. In S. Albrecht (Ed.), *Handbook of Employee Engagement* (pp. 20–30). Edward Elgar.

Kalu, K. A. (2010). National culture and leadership: Followers' preference of transformational or transactional leadership in a power distance culture. *Dissertation Abstracts International Section A: Humanities and Social Sciences, 71*(11-A), 4082.

Lai, A. (2011). *Transformational-Transactional leadership theory.* 2011 AHS Capstone Projects. Paper 17. http://digitalcommons.olin.edu/ahs_capstone_2011/17. Accessed 21 June 2024.

Laschinger, H. K. S., & Finegan, J. (2005). Empowering nurses for work engagement and health in hospital settings. *JONA: The Journal of Nursing Administration, 35*(10), 439–449.

Laschinger, H. K. S., Leiter, M., Day, A., & Gilin, D. (2009). Workplace empowerment, incivility, and burnout: Impact on staff nurse recruitment and retention outcomes. *Journal of Nursing Management, 17*(3), 302–311. https://doi.org/10.1111/j.1365-2834.2009.00999.x

Leitão, C. F., Gomes, V. G., dos santos, D. C., & Maia, B. M. (2023). Innovation and performance in Portuguese hotel sector. *Journal of Tourism & Development, 41*, 551–571. https://doi.org/10.34624/rtd.v4li0.30618

Martinovski, B., Traum, D., & Marsella, S. (2007). Rejection of empathy in negotiation. *Group Decision & Negotiation, 16*(1), 61–76.

Maslow, A. (1970). *Motivation and personality* (2nd ed.). Harper and Row.

Mat-Artun, D., & Küskü, F. (2024). Exploring dual narratives of supervisory trust in remote supervisor–subordinate relationships. *International Social Science Journal.*

Mayer, R. C., Davis, J. H., & Schoorman, F. D. (1995). An integrative model of organizational trust. *Academy of Management Review, 20*(3), 709–734.

Mayer, R., & Gavin, M. (2005). Trust in management and performance: Who minds the shop while employees watch the boss? *Academy of Management Journal, 48*, 874–888.

Mikkelson, A. C., Sloan, D., & Tietsort, C. J. (2021). Employee perceptions of supervisor communication competence and associations with supervisor credibility. *Communication Studies, 72*(4), 600–617. https://doi.org/10.1080/10510974.2021.1953093

Mikkelson, A., Sloan, D., Walter, R., & Hinnenkamp, C. (2024). Supervisor communication competence and employee outcomes: Predictive effects in remote, hybrid, and in-person workplaces. *Business and Professional Communication Quarterly, 87*(3), 462–487. https://doi.org/10.1177/232949062 31167176

Oldham, J. R. (2022). Managers' Resistance to Supervising Teleworking Employees. Digital Commons @ ACU, Electronic Theses and Dissertations. Paper 530. https://digitalcommons.acu.edu/etd/530

Padmakumar, P. A., & Dwivedi, S. (2021). A study of the relationship between transactional leadership style and employee performance in case of private sector in Oman. *International Journal of Scientific Development and Research, 6*(4), 284–290.

Parker, S. K., Knight, C., & Keller, A. (2020). Remote managers are having trust issues. *Harvard Business Review, 30*, 6–20.

Patel, T., Hamlin, R. G., & Louis, D. (2022). Toward a generic framework of negative manager/leader behavior: A comparative study across nations and private sector industries. *European Management Review*, 1–17, https://doi.org/10.1111/emre.12507

Patrick, N. (2023). *The relationship between transactional leadership and its impact on the mental health of subordinates*. Dissertation Abstracts International: Section B: The Sciences and Engineering (Vol. 85, Issue 6-B).

Pearson, C. M., & Porath, C. L. (2005). On the nature, consequences and remedies of workplace incivility: No time for "nice"? Think Again. *Academy of Management Perspectives, 19*(1), 7–18.

Pedraja-Rejas, L., Rodríguez-Ponce, E., Delgado-Almonte, M., & Rodríguez-Ponce, J. (2006). Transformational and transactional leadership: A study of their influence in small companies. *Revista Chilena De Ingeniería, 14*(2), 159–166.

Peng, X. (2023). Advancing workplace civility: A systematic review and meta-analysis of definitions, measurements, and associated factors. *Frontiers in Psychology, 14*, 1277188. https://doi.org/10.3389/fpsyg.2023.1277188

Pennanen, A. (2022). Best practices playbook: Supervisor work in a hybrid work model. Master's thesis, Laurea University of Applied Sciences.www.theseus.fi.

Politis, J. D. (2002). Transformational and transactional leadership enabling (disabling) knowledge acquisition of self-managed teams: The consequences for performance. *Leadership & Organization Development Journal, 23*(4), 186–197.

Porath, C. L., & Gerbasi, A. (2015). Does civility pay? *Organizational Dynamics, 44*(4), 281–286. https://doi.org/10.1016/j.orgdyn.2015.09.005

Porath, C. L., Gerbasi, A., & Schorch, S. L. (2015). The effects of civility on advice, leadership, and performance. *Journal of Applied Psychology, 100*(5), 1527–1541.

Potosky, D., & Azan, W. (2023). Leadership behaviors and human agency in the valley of despair: A meta-framework for organizational change implementation. *Human Resource Management Review, 33*, 100927. https://doi.org/10.1016/j.hrmr.2022.100927

Powell, G. N., Butterfield, D. A., Alves, J. C., & Bartol, K. M. (2004). Sex effects in evaluations of transformational and transactional leaders. *Academy of Management Proceedings*, E1-E6. Academy of Management.

Rawat, P. S., Bhattacharjee, S. B., & Ganesh, V. (2020). Selective incivility, trust and general well-being: A study of women at workplace. *Journal of Indian Business Research, 12*(3), 303–326.

Rahman, M. S., Ferdausy, S., & Bhattacharjee, S. (2014). Assessing the relationships among transformational leadership, transactional leadership, job performance, and gender: An empirical study. *ABAC Journal, 34*(3), 71–91.

Rahman, W. A. W. A. (2016). Empathy and trust: Into a better workplace environment. *Journal of Business and Economics, 7*(12), 2025–2034. https://doi.org/10.15341/jbe(2155-7950)/12.07.2016/009

Rhoades, L., & Eisenberger, R. (2002). Perceived organizational support: A review of the literature. *Journal of Applied Psychology, 87*(4), 698–714. https://doi.org/10.1037/0021-9010.87.4.698

Rockstuhl, T., Wu, D., Dulebohn, J. H., Liao, C., & Hoch, J. E. (2023). Cultural congruence or compensation? A meta-analytic test of transformational and transactional leadership effects across cultures. *Journal of International Business Studies, 54*(3), 476–504.

Sadaqat, S., Abid, G., & Contreras, F. (2022). Influence of contextual factors on turnover intention: Examining the mediating role of civility. *Cogent Business & Management, 9*(1), 2154987. https://doi.org/10.1080/23311975.2022.2154987

Sarkisian, L. M. (2022). *Effective management in the post-pandemic hybrid workplace* [Undergraduate honors thesis]. Bryant Digital Repository. https://digitalcommons.bryant.edu

Schuster, M. (2024). Studies on remote work: challenges and implications for hybrid work arrangements (Doctoral dissertation, Rheinland-Pfälzische Technische Universität Kaiserslautern-Landau)

Shahin, A. I., & Wright, P. L. (2004). Leadership in the context of culture: An Egyptian perspective. *Leadership & Organization Development Journal, 25*(5/6), 499–511. https://doi.org/10.1108/01437730410556743

Shuck, B., & Herd, A. M. (2012). Employee engagement and leadership development: Exploring the convergence of two frameworks and implications for leadership development in HRD. *Human Resource Development Review, 11*(2), 156–181. https://doi.org/10.1177/1534484312438211

Sokolic, D. (2022). Remote work and hybrid work organizations. In M. A. da silva Costa, T. Susak, & V. Haluga (Eds.), *Proceedings of the 78th International*

Scientific Conference on Economic and Social Development (pp. 202–213). Varazdin Development and Entrepreneurship Agency.

Stephens, J. P., Heaphy, E., & Dutton, J. (2011). High-quality connections. In K. Cameron & G. Spreitzer (Eds.), *Handbook of Positive Organizational Scholarship* (pp. 439–448). Oxford University Press.

Tager, M. (2004). What people really need from a change leader. *Leader to Leader, 31,* 6–9.

Tate, R., & White, J. (2005). *People leave managers… **not** organizations! Action-based leadership.* iUniverse.

Wang, G., Oh, I., Courtright, S., & Colbert, A. (2011). Transformational leadership and performance across criteria and levels: A meta-analytic review of 25 years of research. *Group & Organization Management, 36*(2), 223–270. https://doi.org/10.1177/1059601111401017

Wiesenfeld, B. M., Raghuram, S., & Garud, R. (2001). Organizational identification among virtual workers: The role of need for affiliation and perceived work-based social support. *Journal of Management, 27*(2), 213–229. https://doi.org/10.1016/S0149-2063(00)00096-9

Yanchus, N. J., Periard, D., & Osatuke, K. (2017). Further examination of predictors of turnover intention among mental health professionals. *Journal of Psychiatric and Mental Health Nursing, 24*(1), 41–56.

CHAPTER 7

Effective, Caring Leaders

Abstract This chapter describes leaders who are effective as supervisors. They also care about their subordinates, having empathy for them. They go beyond just a respectful relationship with subordinates to a caring, supportive one. Managerial caring involves leaders having an emotional interest in their direct reports and caring authentically about their development. Effective, caring leaders create stronger cultures where employees feel connected, leading to lower turnover and higher performance.

Keywords Effective leaders · Caring leaders · Managerial caring · Empathy

At this level, the leader is effective at being a supervisor. Effective leaders would be at level 5 in empathy (Baron-Cohen, 2011). They are careful not to be intrusive or dominate. They are supportive and consultative. They are also interested in their direct reports' feelings and opinions. They care about their direct reports. They try to find out what motivates them, they attempt to coach them, they give them feedback more than once a year, and they give them recognition when they do an excellent job. They are effective at supervision.

© The Author(s), under exclusive license to Springer Nature Switzerland AG 2025
B. W. Eversole, *The Leadership Spectrum*,
https://doi.org/10.1007/978-3-031-73557-8_7

Effective Leader Behaviors

According Hamlin et al. (2023), the effective supervisor exhibits these behaviors (*as perceived by employees*): "supporting and motivating staff: assists staff personally when they are overloaded with work and/or facing difficult work-based situations; values and gives recognition to staff who achieve; delegates well and empowers (staff); shows *care* for the personal well-being and development of staff: shows *care* by providing understanding and sensitive help and support to staff stressed by difficult personal issues; actively *supports* staff in identifying and meeting their learning and development; exhibits open, trusting, consulting and inclusive behavior: personal approach and open/trusting relationship with staff; involves staff in decision-making and/or consults with them to elicit their opinions/views; communicating with staff and keeping them well informed: keeping staff well informed on matters affecting them; listening to and communicating well with staff and exchanging ideas." This caring and effective leader can be trained and developed to be a leader with a coaching mindset.

Effective managers also appreciate, praise, and recognize their direct reports for a job well done (Hamlin et al., 2023). Comments included, "my manager said, 'I just want to thank you so much,' 'You are a good catch,' 'You've done the right thing,' 'You guys don't know how good you are;' and 'Hey, I heard from so-and-so that you are doing "y" really well'"; and "my manager thanked me for my efforts"; "my manager told me I have done a job well"; "my manager complimented me on a task I exceeded expectations on"; "my manager presented me with a hero of the week award for donating office equipment to the organization"; "my manager told me a workshop I did was a well-run workshop"; and "my manager recognized the value of my input and gave me an appropriate and creative gift."

Effective managers also listen to their direct reports and are honest (Hamlin et al., 2023). Comments included: "on taking up his new appointment, the manager listened to a staff member regarding an issue, which he said he would fix," "when I approach my manager, he is always available," "when I approach my manager, he listens and asks questions," "my manager creates a culture where he listens to staff and is open," "my manager listened to my request," "my manager listens to others but keeps an open mind," and "my manager listens well, encourages discussion." Also, "my manager is honest and straightforward," "my manager is reliable and keeps promises," and "my manager keeps confidences."

In my own research with Hamlin (unpublished manuscript) on effective leader behaviors with subordinates, I have heard employees say the following that demonstrated that their manager cared about their well-being: "my manager suggested that we should not work late so we could go home to our families"; "my manager understands me and *cares* for my well-being"; "my manager *supported* me through difficult family times"; "my manager is flexible with my work hours, knowing that I will get my work done; my manager regularly approaches staff to see how they are doing"; "my manager *supported* me and gave me what I needed when I had personal struggles"; "my manager reduced my workload to help me manage my stress"; and "my manager released me from a line responsibility to reduce my stress."

Caring about your employees as a leader while also paying attention to the bottom line is becoming more and more expected (Depow et al., 2023). Leadership should include caring for others (Ciulla, 2009). Barsade et al. (2003) coined the term "affective revolution" to describe the claim that emotions have become more accepted and even important in the workplace. Leaders have a great influence over the welfare of their subordinates (Montano et al., 2023) meaning they should be emotionally involved with them (Rosete & Ciarrochi, 2005). Emotional intelligence and understanding their subordinates' emotions is an important skill for leaders (Kock et al., 2019).

Sutton (2012) notes that "best bosses" have humanity and provide their employees with dignity and pride. As he also noted, "As over fifty years of research shows, treating employees with respect, encouraging them to participate and to make suggestions, and listening to them are as important as ever. The same is true about setting a clear direction, making decisions, and taking charge" (p. 263).

Csikszentmihalyi (2004) describes what a manager needs to do to build an organization that will retain people who will contribute: make the workplace attractive; make the job valuable and meaningful; and select and reward individuals who will find job satisfaction in their work. He goes on to state that leaders need to provide clear goals, relevant feedback, match job challenges to workers' skills, and provide a sense of autonomy and flexibility to their subordinates to make work that will flow, allowing happy and productive workers.

Sutton's (2012) great bosses have five characteristics. They tread the fine line between being too assertive and not assertive enough, and never micromanage. They also treat the work as a marathon, persistently and patiently moving forward. They also focus on small wins, which are realistic and not too difficult. They avoid doing things that undermine their direct reports' performance and dignity. Finally, great bosses have their subordinates' backs. They don't blame them for their own mistakes, they protect them, *care* for them, and fight for them. The best leaders are both competent and benevolent.

MANAGERIAL CARING

Effective bosses have caring relationships with their direct reports (Galliard, 2019). This brings out their employees' best efforts. A caring relationship means looking for developmental opportunities and putting employees in situations where they can be successful. Having a caring relationship also means that you are aware of both significant milestones and challenges in your employees' lives. Leaders need to celebrate the milestones and be flexible with the challenges. Finally, a caring relationship with your subordinates means you treat them with respect, do not demean them, do what you say you are going to do, and never break confidences with them. This will help build not only a caring relationship, but a trusting one. Moreover, effective leaders who show concern for their direct reports are more likely to obtain the behaviors from them that they would like (Yukl, 2013).

Managerial caring goes further than just caring about direct reports, it involves a leader having an authentic interest in them and their development (Coyne, as cited in Carmeli et al., 2016). In fact, Bass and Avolio (1994) noted when leaders cared as much about the development of their subordinates as they did about them getting their tasks done successfully, their organizations' culture would be the most developed and mature. Leaders may also develop an emotional connection with their direct reports (Skovholt, 2005). Kroth and Keeler (2009) conceptualized managerial caring as a recursive process, with behaviors occurring over time, leading to a growth of care between the leader and their subordinate. In a study of generational effects, Sessa et al. (2007) found that older generations ranked caring more important than determination and ambition as leadership characteristics; yet younger generations still valued a leader who was individually caring more than older generations did. (For a full discussion of managerial caring as a construct and leader-member-exchange (LMX) see Kroth and Keeler [2009]).

Stallard (2020) suggests that effective leaders build a connection culture, noting that connection increases well-being, wellness, and performance. Employees who feel committed are 87% less likely to turnover and their performance is 20% better (CLC, 2004). In a connected culture, employees feel that they have a shared positive vision, that they're valued as humans, and they have a voice (Stallard, 2020).

Kerns' (2021) teaching leaders are also caring leaders. They are "wise warmly assertive caregiving leaders" (Kerns, 2020; Rath, 2020) who care for others, make wise decisions, and project strength. Their motives are transcendent, they have a meaningful calling, and want to help others be their best. Reed (1994) introduced the concept of the *caring* leader. "The caring leader is trusting and honest, is friendly in their personal relationships, shares praise and gives credit where it is due, is an active listener, creates teams, is a mentor and teacher, helps and shares with peers, uses power but does so very carefully, and is an analytical decision-maker" (p. 259). Effective, caring leaders are also supportive leaders (Prentice, 2022). Supportive leaders improve both job satisfaction and employee engagement in organizations.

Ellinger and Bostrom (2002) conducted research with managers about caring attitudes and if all managers possessed them. Here are a few of their comments from the study:

M12 (one of the participants in the study) said:

> I honestly, sincerely care about people and the people I work with in particular, and you know, you can be the biggest jackass in the world, but if you really *care* about people, people know that, they can sniff it out and so I think that helped me out. (p. 162)

M1 said:

> So, my philosophy is, I'm here to help you. I guess if I were to boil it down to one thing, and they have to believe that I am here to help them. (p. 163)

Similarly, M5 said,

You have to *care* about people. I think that some people can be very good at facilitating learning and some people don't care to be. A lot is the individual, how you were brought up. I believe that. Some people are just good people, and some people really aren't, OK, or their motivation is to get to the top of the ladder in this company, or whatever company that is, and they don't care. They really don't. (p. 163)

Sutton (2012) gave an example of an employee with an effective, caring boss. She made a five-minute fund-raising appeal at her store for her boss, and told Sutton, "I hate most managers; I wouldn't do a thing for them. But I love Dave and I will do whatever he asks" (p. 20). Imagine the engagement in organizations if all managers were like Dave!

GENDER AND EFFECTIVE, CARING LEADERS

As noted in Chapter 1, there is a paucity of women in senior leadership positions. One reason is that women are less likely than men to seek out leadership positions (Bierema, 2016; Brands & Fernandez-Mateo, 2017; Ryan et al., 2016; Fernandez-Mateo & Fernandez, 2016) despite the fact that the underrepresentation of women as leaders actually harms organizations (Zenger & Folkman, 2019), especially as women are less likely to commit ethical breaches (Casal, 2013). The 32 companies in the S&P 500 currently run by women CEOs have done substantially better than those with men CEOs (468 companies) (Personal Finance Club, 2024). Moreover, according to the same club, over the past decade, organizations led by women returned 384% while for organizations led by men the return was 261%.

Women often demonstrate care in their relationships, however regarding the likelihood to use managerial care, there does not seem to be a strong difference between men and women (Jaffee & Shibley-Hyde, 2000; Simola et al., 2010). Nevertheless, research suggests that although women and men have equivalent leadership skills and qualifications, both men and women subordinates tend to prefer men as leaders (Eagly & Karau, 2002; Tahmincioglu, 2007). However, Fischer et al. (2023) caution against leadership effectiveness studies that do not measure effectiveness directly in terms of behavior. Perceptions of behavior, the actual behavior itself, and their evaluation need to be well-differentiated before making conclusions about gender and leadership effectiveness (Gerpott et al., 2024). According to Yan et al. (2018), "…existing studies have not yet reached a consensus on the issue of whether females are more or less convincing than males in terms of their leadership effectiveness" (p. 107). Her study of men and women presidents in the U.S. and China found no differences in leadership effectiveness.

Yet it is still considered to be typical culturally that women, rather than men, are considerate, supportive, and caring (Eagly & Carli, 2007). Gerzema and D'Antonio (2013) wrote, "the world would be a better place if more men thought like women" (p. 9) after their global research in 13 countries that suggested intuition, empathy, and collaboration (which they noted were feminine traits) would be important for future leaders.

Culture and Effective, Caring Leaders

Hamlin and his colleagues have conducted multiple studies in multiple countries worldwide and have found that the behaviors that make leaders effective with their subordinates have been largely the same (Hamlin et al., 2012; Hamlin et al., 2023; Patel et al., 2022). A recent study by Lerutla and Steyn (2022) in South Africa came to the same conclusion, finding that "Thus, those African and Western cultural backgrounds act similarly, and the outcomes (effectiveness) was comparable" (p. 1). Hanges et al. (2016) likewise noted that the 2014 GLOBE (Global Leadership and Organizational Behavioral Effectiveness) study showed that "culture did not directly influence actual leader behavior or leadership effectiveness" (p. 66). Moreover, Posner (2013) concluded

> The more frequently that leaders engage in the five practices of exemplary leaders, whether in Ethiopia, India, Pakistan, or the Philippines, or elsewhere, the more effective they will be, even if the degree to which they are so engaged may vary from one country (culture) to another. The findings echo what many executives, like Wang (2010) and Peshawaria (2011) maintain, that effective leadership looks much more similar than different around the globe. (p. 584)

However, cultural differences may affect direct report ratings due to power distance. Agrawal and Rook (2014) studied INSEAD students from 128 nations and found that direct reports from the East rated their leaders higher (using a 360-degree assessment) on most dimensions on the Global Executive Leadership Inventory, (GELI) including emotional intelligence, than direct reports of Western leaders. Kossek et al. (2017) studied the effects of cross-cultural raters of leadership effectiveness particularly and found that power distance could bias ratings.

Morrison and Black (2014) claim that global leaders must establish empathetic relationships with subordinates in order to be effective. This includes listening to others, which comes with some potential cultural barriers. These include the two erroneous assumptions that everyone either already does or should think the same way as the leader does, or that the leader has communication barriers in language or culture. Some examples are that in Japan the same word means "yes" and "no"; and in the Middle East, women managers may not want to shake hands with a man. Deardorff (2006) similarly noted the importance of empathy in their model of intercultural competence. Pusch (2009) described these skills as cross-cultural empathy:

> being able to participate in another person's experience in your imagi-
> nation; thinking it intellectually and feeling it emotionally. The ability to
> connect emotionally with people and showing compassion for others, being
> able to listen actively and mindfully, and viewing situations from more than
> one perspective is an important set of skills that demonstrate empathy.
> (p. 70)

Kouzes and Posner (2011) did a study of over 75,000 employees globally and found that caring was one of the top-rated traits of admired leaders. Gabriel (2015) goes so far as to argue "Leaders, I shall argue, will always be judged by their followers against their ability to demonstrate that they care" (p. 317). Nevertheless, in Western culture care is generally not practiced by leaders but by underpaid and devalued underprivileged and marginalized groups such as in care homes, schools, and hospitals (e.g., Tronto, 1993).

CONCLUSION

Effective, caring leaders are supportive and demonstrate care and concern for their direct reports. These leaders bring out the best efforts from their employees. While civil leaders and caring, effective leaders use a transactional leadership style and may even use transformational styles, the next level on the continuum uses a transformational leadership style to lead with a coaching mindset.

REFERENCES

Agrawal, A., & Rook, C. (2014). Global leaders in East and West: Do all global leaders lead in the same way? In J. S. Osland, M. Li, & Y. Wang (Eds.), *Advances in global leadership* (pp. 155–179). Emerald Group Publishing Limited.

Baron-Cohen, S. (2011). *The science of evil: On empathy and the origins of cruelty.* Basic Books.

Barsade, S., Brief, A. P., Spataro, S. E., & Greenberg, J. (2003). The affective revolution in organizational behavior: The emergence of a paradigm. *Organizational behavior: A management challenge, 1,* 3–50.

Bass, B. M., & Avolio, B. J. (1994). Transformational leadership and organizational culture. *The International Journal of Public Administration, 17*(3–4), 541–554.

Bierema, L. L. (2016). Women's leadership: Troubling notions of the "ideal" (male) leader. *Advances in Developing Human Resources, 18*(2), 119–136.

Brands, R. A., & Fernandez-Mateo, I. (2017). Leaning out: How negative recruitment experiences shape women's decisions to compete for executive roles. *Administrative Science Quarterly, 62*(3), 405–442. https://www.jstor.org/stable/44508558

Carmeli, A., Jones, C. D., & Binyamin, G. (2016). The power of caring and generativity in building strategic adaptability. *Journal of Occupational and Organizational Psychology, 89*(1), 46–72.

Casal, P. (2013). Sexual dimorphism and human enhancement. *Journal of Medical Ethics, 39*(12), 722–728.

Ciulla, J. B. (2009). Leadership and the ethics of care. *Journal of Business Ethics, 88,* 3–4.

CLC (2004). *Driving performance and retention through employee engagement.* Corporate Executive Board.

Csikszentmihalyi, M. (2004). *Good business: Leadership, flow, and the making of meaning.* Penguin.

Deardorff, D. K. (2006). Identification and assessment of intercultural competence as a student outcome of internationalization. *Journal of Studies in Intercultural Education, 10,* 241–266.

Depow, G. J., Hobson, N. M., Beck, J., Inzlicht, M., & Hougaard, R. (2023, June 1). The compassion advantage: Leaders who care outperform leaders who share followers' emotions. https://doi.org/10.31234/osf.io/md2g8

Eagly, A. H., & Carli, L. L. (2007). Women and the labyrinth of leadership. *Harvard Business Review, 85*(9), 63–71.

Eagly, A. H., & Karau, S. J. (2002). Role of congruity theory of prejudice toward female leaders. *Psychological Review, 109*(3), 573–598.

Ellinger, A. D., & Bostrom, R. P. (2002). An examination of managers' beliefs about their roles as facilitators of learning. *Management Learning, 33*(2), 147–179.

Fernandez-Mateo, I., & Fernandez, R. M. (2016). Bending the pipeline? Executive search and gender inequality in hiring for top management jobs. *Management Science, 62*(12), 3636–3655. https://www.jstor.org/stable/44166545

Fischer, T., Hambrick, D. C., Sajons, G. B., & Van Quaquebeke, N. (2023). Leadership science beyond questionnaires. *The Leadership Quarterly, 34*(6), 101752. https://doi.org/10.1016/j.leaqua.2023.101752

Gabriel, Y. (2015). The caring leader–what followers expect of their leaders and why? *Leadership, 11*(3), 316–334. https://doi.org/10.1177/1742715014532482

Galliard, A. (2019). *Care to lead.* Archangel Ink.

Gerpott, F. H., Gloor, J. L., Neely, B. H., Jr., & Tonidandel, S. (2024). Special issue call on gender and leadership: Taking stock and two steps forward. *The Leadership Quarterly, 35*, 101787.

Gerzema, J., & D'Antonio, M. (2013). *The Athena doctrine: How women (and men who think like them) will rule the future.* Jossey-Bass.

Hamlin, R. G., Patel, T., Ruiz, C., & Whitford, S. (2012). Towards a universal taxonomy of perceived managerial and leadership effectiveness: A multiple cross-case/cross-nation study of effective and ineffective managerial behaviour. In *Proceedings of the 13th UFHRD International Conference of Human Resource Development Research and Practice across Europe.* UFHRD.

Hamlin, R. G., Ruiz, C. E., Jones, J., & Patel, T. (2023). Toward a universalistic behavioral model of perceived managerial and leadership effectiveness for the health services sector. *Health Services Management Research, 36*(2), 89–101. https://doi.org/10.1177/09514848211065462

Hanges, P. J., Aiken, J. R., Park, J., & Su, J. (2016). Cross-cultural leadership: Leading around the world. *Current Opinion in Psychology, 8*, 64–69.

Jaffee, S., & Shibley-Hyde, J. (2000). Gender differences in moral orientation: A meta-analysis. *Psychological Bulletin, 126*, 703–726.

Kerns, C. D. (2020). Managing wisdom: A practice-oriented leadership framework. *Journal of Management Policy & Practice, 21*(5), 9–27.

Kerns, C. D. (2021). Bad leaders: Some realities, reasons and remedies. In A. Örtenblad (Ed.), *Debating Bad Leadership: Reasons and Remedies* (pp. 219–234). Palgrave Macmillan.

Kock, N., Mayfield, M., Mayfield, J., Sexton, S., & De La Garza, L. M. (2019). Empathetic leadership: How leader emotional support and understanding influences follower performance. *Journal of Leadership & Organizational Studies, 26*(2), 217–236.

Kossek, E. E., Huang, J. L., Piszczek, M. M., Fleenor, J. W., & Ruderman, M. (2017). Rating expatriate leader effectiveness in multisource feedback systems: Cultural distance and hierarchical effects. *Human Resource Management*, 56(1), 151–172.

Kouzes, J. M., & Posner, B. (2011). *Credibility: How leaders gain and lose it, why people demand it* (2nd ed.). Jossey-Bass. https://doi.org/10.1002/978 1118983867

Kroth, M., & Keeler, C. (2009). Caring as a managerial strategy. *Human Resource Development Review*, 8(4), 506–531.

Lerutla, M., & Steyn, R. (2022). Distinct leadership styles and differential effectiveness across culture: An analysis of South African business leaders. *South African Journal of Human Resource Management*, 20, 1–11.

Montano, D., Schleu, J. E., & Hüffmeier, J. (2023). A meta-analysis of the relative contribution of leadership styles to followers' mental health. *Journal of Leadership & Organizational Studies*, 30(1), 90–107. https://doi.org/10. 1177/15480518221114854

Morrison, A. J., & Black, J. S. (2014). The character of global leaders. In *Advances in global leadership* (Vol. 8, pp. 183–204). Emerald Group Publishing Limited.

Patel, T., Hamlin, R. G., & Louis, D. (2022). Toward a generic framework of negative manager/leader behavior: A comparative study across nations and private sector industries. *European Management Review*, 1–17, https://doi. org/10.1111/emre.12507

Personal finance club.com (2024). *Are female CEOs better than male CEOs*. https://www.personalfinanceclub.com/are-female-ceos-better-than-male-ceos/. Accessed 18 July 2024.

Peshawaria, R. (2011, May 16). Leading across borders? Don't change a thing. http://blogs.hbr.org/cs/2011/05/leading_across_borders_dont_ch. html. Accessed 28 October 2024.

Posner, B. Z. (2013). It's how leaders behave that matters, not where they are from. *Leadership & Organization Development Journal*, 34(6), 573–587. https://doi.org/10.1108/LODJ-11-2011-0115

Prentice, S. B. (2022). Job satisfaction or employee engagement: Regardless of which comes first, supportive leadership improves them both. *Advances in Developing Human Resources*, 24(4), 275–285. https://doi.org/10.1177/ 15234223221112504

Pusch, M. D. (2009). The interculturally competent global leader. In D. K. Deardorff (Ed.), *The SAGE handbook of intercultural competence* (pp. 66–84). Sage.

Rath, T. (2020). *Life's great question: Discover how you contribute to the world*. Silicon Guild Books.

Reed, S. F. (1994). *The toxic executive: A step-by-step guide for turning your boss (or yourself) from noxious to nurturing.* Harper Business.

Rosete, D., & Ciarrochi, J. (2005). Emotional intelligence and its relationship to workplace performance outcomes of leadership effectiveness. *Leadership & Organization Development Journal, 26*(5), 388–399.

Ryan, M. K., Haslam, S. A., Morgenroth, T., Rink, F., Stoker, J., & Peters, K. (2016). Getting on top of the glass cliff: Reviewing a decade of evidence, explanations, and impact. *The Leadership Quarterly, 27*(3), 446–455.

Sessa, V. I., Kabacoff, R. I., Deal, J., & Brown, H. (2007). Generational differences in leader values and leadership behaviors. *The Psychologist-Manager Journal, 10*(1), 47–74.

Skovholt, T. M. (2005). The cycle of caring: A model of expertise in the helping professions. *Journal of Mental Health Counseling, 27*(1), 82–93.

Simola, S. K., Barling, J., & Turner, N. (2010). Transformational leadership and leader moral orientation: Contrasting an ethic of justice and an ethic of care. *The Leadership Quarterly, 21*(1), 179–188. https://doi.org/10.1016/j.leaqua.2009.10.013

Stallard, M. L. (2020). *Connection culture* (2nd ed.). ATD.

Sutton, R. I. (2012). *Good boss, bad boss: How to be the best... and learn from the worst.* Business Plus.

Tahmincioglu, E. (2007, March 6). *Men rule—At least in workplace attitudes.* Elle/MSNBC.com survey. www.msnbc.com/id/17345308. Accessed 15 July 2024.

Tronto, J. C. (1993). *Moral boundaries: A political argument for an ethic of care.* Routledge.

Wang, C. (2010). *Managerial decision making and leadership.* John Wiley & Sons.

Yukl, G. (2013). *Leadership in organizations* (8th ed.). Pearson.

Yan, S., Wu, Y., & Zhang, G. (2018). The gender difference in leadership effectiveness and its Sino-US comparison. *Chinese Management Studies, 12*(1), 106–124. https://doi.org/10.1108/CMS-07-2016-0148

Zenger, J., & Folkman, J. (2019). *Research: Women score higher than men in most leadership skills.* https://hbr.org/2019/06/research-women-score-higher-than-men-in-most-leadership-skills. Accessed 10 February 2024.

CHAPTER 8

Coaching Mindset Transformational Leader

Abstract This chapter describes the leader with a coaching mindset who leads with a transformational style. This leader has a good amount of empathy for their subordinates which they use to coach them. Managerial coaches are also high in emotional intelligence. Subordinates of coaches using transformational leadership experience increased engagement, satisfaction, and performance.

Keywords Manager as coach · Managerial coaching · Transformational leaders · Emotional intelligence · Empathy

COACHING

Leaders today have been exhorted to be coaches with their people (Sonthalia, 2024). They are being advised to demur from giving answers and instead make enquiries; to provide support for their employees rather than evaluate them; and to focus on development rather than command and control in their management (Ibarra & Scoular, 2019). In one survey in 2018, a third of companies in 2018 have trained their managers in how to use coaching in the management of their people (Filipkowski et al., 2018). So, what is all the fuss about?

Defined

This level of leader is near the end of the spectrum and is close to the Super Empathetic leader. They would be at Level 5 of Baron-Cohen's (2011) empathy curve. They are focused on the emotions of their direct reports, checking on them and supporting them when needed. They have a coaching mindset and try to find out what is motivating to their direct report and then try to provide that to them. Dweck and Leggett (1988) described those with growth mindsets as having assumptions that others (as well as themselves) are capable of development and change; this assumption guides their relationships and their own behavior. Sonthalia (2024) defined the coaching mindset as "an open, curious, flexible, and client-centred attitude" (p. 1).

However, this emphasis on manager as coach is nothing new. Back in 2002, over 20 years ago, Hunt and Weintraub had this to say about leaders with a coaching mindset:

> YOU know who they are. The executives or managers down the hall or across the parking lot that everybody seems to love to work for. Somehow their people always end up getting the plum assignments. And the CEO loves them because they always seem to have the best people working for them, people who end up going places in the company. Secretly, you feel jealous. Every so often you'll overhear one of your own employees whispering to a friend, "I'd give my right arm to be working for them." ...Managers who coach, who actively help their employees learn and grow, are seen by their employees and others as leaders who make significant contributions. They are superior business managers who coach not just to be altruistic but to generate business results. They often have lower than expected turnover in their ranks, except when their employees leave to step up to more significant roles along their career paths. Other employees want to work for coaching managers because they believe, rightly, that working for a coaching manager will ultimately enhance their careers. (p. 39)

Traits

A leader with a coaching mindset, according to Hunt and Weintraub (as cited in Ellinger et al., 2018) has empathy and wants to help others develop; they believe that others want to learn; want to help; are open to getting feedback and learning about themselves; and although they have high standards, they do not have a high need for control. Managers with a coaching mindset want to develop and grow people, empowering, helping, supporting, and removing obstacles (Ellinger & Bostrom, 2002).

Hunt and Weintraub (2002) offered these guidelines for managers who want to be coaches: "They have a coaching mindset" (p. 42); they generate an environment that is conducive to coaching; before giving any feedback, they are sure to inquire about what is going on first, and then pay attention to what their direct reports are saying, and only then give specific feedback that is appropriate to the situation; and they don't quit. Having a coaching mindset means believing that your direct reports can, and want to, learn. An environment conducive to coaching is one where it is okay to fail and be open—which is what learning requires. Only giving feedback after your employees have had a chance to contemplate and evaluate their own situation first allows them to create their own notions and solutions first. Managers who are coaches are always aware of the skills and abilities that their people are developing and are constantly working with them to do so.

Ladyshewsky (2010) described the manager as coach:

> The MAC [manager as coach] role is quite distinct from the traditional coaching role where the coach's only role is to support an individual in their professional and/or personal development. The MAC does use a coaching approach with his/her staff, but this role is not their main function. The MAC who adopts this coaching role as part of their skill base rejects the command-and-control model of leadership. Instead, the MAC builds a relationship around trust and believes in the capabilities of the individuals who form part of his/her team. (pp. 293–294)

Managers also need to share values with their employees, which can be accomplished by getting to know them personally (Ladyshewsky, 2010). Perhaps most important is the ability to build trust (Joo, 2005). The supervisor will not be able to do this without shifting from a focus on control to a focus on learning (Ellinger & Bostrom, 2002; Ladyshewsky, 2010). Hurley (2006) also noted that being honest and authentic, self-disclosing, doing what one says one will do, and spending time in the relationship also build trust. Finally, trust cannot be built with a manager who does not have credibility with their direct reports (Ladyshewsky, 2010). This last point underscores the notion that empathy (required for the manager as coach) is necessary but not sufficient for the coaching relationship to be successful. The coaching relationship can only be successful if the employee considers the manager capable and competent (Ladyshewsky, 2010)—and empathetic (Beattie, 2002; Goleman, 2000; Goleman et al., 2002; Hunt & Weintraub, 2002; Wasylysyn, 2003).

Emotional intelligence (EI) is also important for the manager as coach (Ladyshewsky, 2010). Those high in EI can use those skills to help others improve their own performance (Goleman et al., 2002). With high EI, managerial coaches not only are able to build the social relationship necessary for coaching their employees, but also understand their own and others' motives as well (Howard, 2006). Coaching is similar to therapy but yet distinct; Żukowska and Miąsek (2014) offer a good analysis.

Behaviors

Ellinger et al. (2018) note that the skills of managerial coaches can be grouped into three main categories: assessing, challenging, and supporting. More specifically, they empower and facilitate (Ellinger, 1997; Ellinger & Bostrom, 2002). Empowering skills include framing questions to help employees evaluate problems; being supportive in clearing hurdles; shifting responsibilities to direct reports; and allowing direct reports to find answers themselves. Facilitating skills include giving and asking for feedback; generating and encouraging an environment conducive to learning and development; getting direct reports to think in alternative ways; working through things together; being sure expectations are conveyed; drawing others into learning experiences; and using imaginative ways to learn. Beattie (2002) offered a similar taxonomy of skills that a managerial coach should have, also including empowering skills as well as empathy, support, and encouragement; developing, coaching, and counseling; sharing information and thinking; giving feedback; and being a role model.

Wasylysyn (2003) noted that managerial coaches need the following skills: empathy, ability to solve problems, active listening, interpersonal abilities, flexibility, and patience. Empathy actually develops when coaches use their active listening skills (Tyler, 2011). Wilson (2007) described five different levels of listening: "waiting for our turn to speak," "giving our own experience," "giving advice," "listening and asking for more," and "intuitive listening" (pp. 20–21).

Self-awareness is an important skill for managerial coaches. In order to be self-aware, a supervisor has to not only understand themselves, but also understand how they are viewed by their subordinates (Taylor, 2010).

Prevalence

Gallup (Robison, 2020) estimates that only about 2 in 10 managers are coaches.

Outcomes

Employee engagement has been increased, as well as intrinsic motivation to reach goals, when supervisors coach their employees (Gruman & Saks, 2011; Xanthopoulou et al., 2009). Engagement-enhancing coaching of employees includes helping with work planning, identifying work challenges, giving emotional support and advice, and instilling self-efficacy or confidence (Schaufeli & Salanova, 2007). As Gruman and Saks (2011) put it, "Engagement facilitation recasts the role of supervisors as coaches whose goal is to design tasks and provide support and resources that energize employees and absorb them in their jobs" (p. 133). Coaching not only improves engagement, but there is evidence that it improves organizational outcomes as well. Elmadag et al. (2008) did a study of 310 frontline employees in the logistics service provider industry and found that managerial coaching had more of an effect on their commitment to service quality than rewards did.

Having a coaching mindset, the leader as coach experiences more sharing of power with subordinates, becomes a facilitator, and perceives their direct reports as more resourceful as opposed to dependent team members (Sonthalia, 2024).

Transformational Leadership

Managerial coaches use a transformational leadership style (Ahrens & McCarthy, 2016). Unlike civil leaders who use a transactional leadership style, transformational leaders go beyond mere transactional exchanges to motivate, inspire, and empower subordinates (Gill, 2002).

Defined

Transformational leaders provide their subordinates with a transcendent motivation that goes beyond their own (Bass, 1985). This leadership style has four dimensions: idealized influence, inspirational motivation, intellectual stimulation, and individualized consideration.

Behaviors

According to Bass and Riggio (2005), transformational leaders act as coaches and mentors, create supportive environments, accept individual needs, and effectively listen to subordinates. They enhance the productivity of their subordinates by transforming their behavior (Burns, 2004). Transformational leaders help increase their subordinates' intrinsic motivation so that they see their work as meaningful and important (Zhu et al., 2009).

This leadership style transforms employees by focusing on their Maslow (1970) needs that are of a higher order: self-esteem and self-actualization, thus encouraging them to accomplish goals greater than what is expected of them (Bass, 1985; Fareed & Su, 2022; Martinez & Leija, 2023). This is done by leaders not only focusing on the needs of their employees, but also on the value of their objectives and the importance of employees going above their own self-interest (Bass, 1985).

Transformational leaders also pay attention to the emotions of their subordinates (Cheng et al., 2023; Eseryel & Eseryel, 2013) and their development (Chen et al., 2022). They are supportive and show concern for their subordinates, and always recognize their achievements (Rafferty & Griffin, 2004). They establish strong relationships with followers and have charisma (Humphreys & Einstein, 2003).

Transformational leaders also use personalized interactions, are committed to shared goals and expectations, and motivate followers using optimism and enthusiasm (Ahrens & McCarthy, 2016). Leaders with a transformational style help build trust and self-efficacy in subordinates (Eseryel & Eseryel, 2013; Potosky & Azan, 2023). Their focus is on not only empowering but engaging their subordinates and listening to them (Potosky & Azan, 2023).

Outcomes

Transformational leaders have the ability to inspire their followers to exceed expectations and increase their abilities (Boerner et al., 2007; Gill, 2002). Judge and Piccolo (2004) and Kalu (2010) found that employees of transformational leaders were more likely to be satisfied and motivated. Employees of transformational leaders are also more likely to be engaged (Azim et al., 2021; Widodo & Mawarto, 2020) and to appreciate and be loyal to them (Yukl, 2013). Subordinates of transformational leaders are also encouraged to learn and explore (Bass & Riggio, 2005) and have a greater sense of empowerment and self-efficacy (Bandura, 2006; Potosky & Azan, 2023).

In studies in the hotel industry, employees of transformational leaders reported less stress and more motivation and satisfaction (Clark et al., 2009; Gill et al., 2006). Studies have shown that transformational leadership is associated with employee satisfaction and improved organizational performance (As-Sadiq & Khoury, 2006; Avolio et al., 2004). Wang et al. (2011) showed that transformational leadership was positively related to subordinate performance. Transformational leadership has been linked to employee positive well-being (Anderson, 2017). However, a combination of transformational and transactional leadership styles may be even more effective, leading to increased follower performance, satisfaction, and motivation (Oke et al., 2012).

Gender and Coaching Transformational Leaders

There isn't much research into the gender of managerial coaches (Beattie et al., 2014; Stout-Rostron et al., 2013). In fact, gender is a controlled variable in many managerial coaching studies (e.g., Zheng et al., 2022). However, women are most likely to exhibit behaviors important to managerial coaching (Wang & Howell, 2012). Women managers are also more likely to exhibit a leadership style that is focused on interpersonal relationships (Anderson et al., 2006; Kark et al., 2012), also important to managerial coaching. Furnham et al. (2023) found that women coaches were preferred over men in their study of 504 professionals. In a global study of 600,000 employees in 51 countries, Ye et al. (2016) found that women leaders were managerial coaches more often than men.

As early as 1996, Bass et al. found that women leaders displayed transformational leadership behaviors more frequently than men did, as rated by both men and women subordinates. Later studies also found that women leaders were more likely to utilize transformational leadership styles than men were (Eagly et al., 2003; Gartzia & van Engen, 2012; Martin, 2015; Simola et al., 2010), while men tended to be transactional (Alimo-Metcalfe, 2004; Powell et al., 2004). In fact, other studies found that women were better at being transformational leaders than men (Kao et al., 2006; van Engen & Willemsen, 2004). In a study by Šiber et al. (2023) in Croatia, women leaders were found to be more transformational and intellectually humble than men.

As a group, women have higher EQ scores than men do (Joseph & Newman, 2010) and those with higher EQs tend to be more effective in leadership roles (Chamorro-Premuzic, 2019). Nevertheless, women still struggle to be perceived as effective as men as leaders. In a study by Rhee and Sigler (2015), men leaders who practiced a participatory style were still rated as more effective than women who did so.

Culture and Coaching Transformational Leaders

Hamlin et al. (2006) also did a cross-cultural analysis of managerial coaching effectiveness studies in the U.S., Scotland, and England and found a high degree of similarity. In a global study of 600,000 employees in 51 countries, Ye et al. (2016) found that men leaders who were managerial coaches were more often influenced by culture than women managerial coaches.

Most managerial coaching studies have been done in Western cultures (Beattie et al., 2014). An exception to this was a study done by Kim et al. (2013) in South Korea, who found relationships between coaching and job performance. A later study by Kim et al. (2014) compared coaching in the U.S. and South Korea and found significant similarities, as well as nearly the same quantity of managerial coaching being experienced in both nations notwithstanding the contrasting culture of the two countries (e.g., power distance and uncertainty avoidance (Hofstede, 1991).

Bass and Riggio (2005) claimed that transformational leadership behaviors transcend national culture, in agreement with Boehnke et al. (2003), Hamlin et al. (2012), and Patel et al. (2022). For example, Jackson et al. (2013) found in their meta-analysis that the relationship between affective commitment to an organization and transformational leadership was not affected by national culture.

However, other studies on transformational leadership in other cultures have had mixed results. Walumbwa et al. (2005) compared transformational leadership in the U.S. and Kenya and found a strong relationship between it and organizational commitment and job satisfaction in both countries. Shahin and Wright (2004) tested this assertion in their study in Egypt, a high power distance country (Hofstede, 1991). They surveyed leaders and their direct reports on transformational leadership and had mixed results. Kalu (2010) did a study in Nigeria, another high power distance country, and found that transformational leadership had a significant relationship with subordinate job satisfaction. However, Cho et al.

(2019) showed that the relationship between transformational leadership and affective organizational commitment was stronger in their U.S. sample than in their Korean one, another high power distance country. Singh et al. (2022) found in a study of 98 employees in India that transformational leaders were more effective than transactional. While Rockstuhl et al. (2023) found that transformational leadership had a more positive effect on performance in high power distance cultures and high collectivist cultures. Jackson et al. (2013) similarly found that in collectivist cultures transformational leadership was more likely to increase employees' normative commitment to the organization.

CONCLUSION

Leaders who use managerial coaching with a transformational leadership style use empathy to help their subordinates achieve superior performance, satisfaction, and well-being. However, according to Barbuto and Wheeler (2006) and Stone et al. (2004), even leaders who use a transformational style to inspire their subordinates are still inspiring their subordinates to pursue organizational goals, while servant leaders are truly focused on their followers rather than the organization. We now turn to the end of the empathy spectrum.

REFERENCES

Ahrens, J., & McCarthy, G. (2016). Managerial coaching: A practical way to apply leadership theory? In P. A. Davis (Ed.), *The Psychology of Effective Coaching and Management* (pp. 353–365). Nova Science Publishers Inc.

Alimo-Metcalfe, B. (2004). Leadership: A masculine past, but a feminine future? *Gender and Excellence in the Making* (pp.161–168). European Commission.

Anderson, M. (2017). Transformational leadership in education: A review of existing literature. *International Social Science Review, 93*(1), 1–13.

Anderson, N., Lievens, F., Van Dam, K., & Born, M. (2006). A construct-driven investigation of gender differences in a leadership-role assessment center. *Journal of Applied Psychology, 91*(3), 555–556. https://doi.org/10.1037/0021-9010.91.3.555

As-Sadiq, H. A., & Khoury, G. C. (2006). Leadership styles in the Palestinian large-scale industrial enterprises. *The Journal of Management Development, 25,* 832–849. https://doi.org/10.1108/02621710610692043

Avolio, B. J., Zhu, W., Koh, W., & Bhatia, P. (2004). Transformational leadership and organizational commitment: Mediating role of psychological empowerment and moderating role of structural distance. *Journal of Organizational Behavior, 25*(8), 951–968. https://doi.org/10.1002/job.283

Azim, M. T., Uddin, M. A., & Haque, M. M. (2021). Does compliance to standards in the ready-made garments industry affect employee attitudes? A study in Bangladesh. *Global Business and Organizational Excellence, 40*(2), 43–58.

Bandura, A. (2006). Toward a psychology of human agency. *Perspectives on Psychological Science, 1*(2), 164–180.

Barbuto, J. E., & Wheeler, D. W. (2006). Scale development and construct clarification of servant leadership. *Group & Organization Management, 31*, 300–326.

Baron-Cohen, S. (2011). *The science of evil: On empathy and the origins of cruelty.* Basic Books.

Bass, B. M. (1985). *Leadership and performance beyond expectations.* The Free Press.

Bass, B. M., Avolio, B. J., & Atwater, L. (1996). The transformational and transactional leadership of men and women. *Applied Psychology, 45*(1), 5–34.

Bass, B. M., & Riggio, R. E. (2005). *Transformational leadership* (2nd ed.). Psychology Press.

Beattie, R. S. (2002). Line managers as facilitators of learning: Empirical evidence from the voluntary sector. *Proceedings of the 2002 Human Resource Development Research and Practice across Europe Conference.* January, 2002. Napier University.

Beattie, R. S., Kim, S., Hagen, M. S., Egan, T. M., Ellinger, A. D., & Hamlin, R. G. (2014). Managerial coaching: A review of the empirical literature and development of a model to guide future practice. *Advances in Developing Human Resources, 16*(2), 184–201. https://doi.org/10.1177/152342231 3520476

Boehnke, K., Bontis, N., DiStefano, J. J., & DiStefano, A. C. (2003). Transformational leadership: An examination of cross-national differences and similarities. *Leadership & Organization Development Journal, 24*(1), 5–15. https://doi.org/10.1108/01437730310457285

Boerner, S., Eisenbeiss, S., & Griesser, D. (2007). Followers' behaviour and organizational performance: The impact of transformational leaders. *Journal of Leadership and Organizational Studies, 13*(3), 15–26. https://doi.org/10.1177/10717919070130030201

Burns, J. M. (2004). *Transforming leadership: A new pursuit of happiness.* Grove Press.

Chamorro-Premuzic, T. (2019). *Why do so many incompetent men become leaders (and how to fix it).* Harvard University Press.

Chen, J., Ghardallou, W., Comite, U., Ahmad, N., Ryu, H. B., Ariza-Montes, A., & Han, H. (2022). Managing hospital employees' burnout through transformational leadership: The role of resilience, role clarity, and intrinsic motivation. *International Journal of Environmental Research and Public Health, 19*(17), 10941.

Cheng, P., Liu, Z., & Zhou, L. (2023). Transformational leadership and emotional labor: The mediation effects of psychological empowerment. *International Journal of Environmental Research and Public Health, 20*(2), 1030.

Cho, Y., Shin, M., Billing, T. K., & Bhagat, R. S. (2019). Transformational leadership, transactional leadership, and affective organizational commitment: A closer look at their relationships in two distinct national contexts. *Asian Business & Management, 18*, 187–210. https://doi.org/10.1057/s41291-019-00059-1

Clark, R., Hartline, M., & Jones, K. (2009). The effects of leadership style on hotel employees' commitment to service quality. *Cornell Hospitality Quarterly, 50*(2), 209–231. https://doi.org/10.1177/1938965508315371

Dweck, C. S., & Leggett, E. L. A. (1988). A social-cognitive approach to motivation and personality. *Psychological Review, 95*(2), 256–273.

Eagly, A. H., Johannesen-Schmidt, M. C., & van Engen, M. L. (2003). Transformational, transactional, and laissez-faire leadership styles: A meta-analysis comparing women and men. *Psychological Bulletin, 129*(4), 569–591. https://doi.org/10.1037/0033-2909.129.4.569

Ellinger, A. M. (1997). *Managers as facilitators of learning in learning organizations* (Publication Number UMI No: 9807100) [Doctoral dissertation, University of Georgia at Athens, GA].

Ellinger, A. D., Beattie, R. S., & Hamlin, R. G. (2018). The manager as coach. In E. Cox, T. Bachkirova, & D. A. Buttercluck (Eds.), *The Complete Handbook of Coaching* (pp. 262–278). Sage.

Ellinger, A. D., & Bostrom, R. P. (2002). An examination of managers' belief about their roles as facilitators of learning. *Management Learning, 33*(2), 147–179.

Elmadag, A. B., Ellinger, A. E., & Franke, G. R. (2008). Antecedents and consequences of frontline service employee commitment to service quality. *Journal of Marketing Theory and Practice, 16*(2), 95–110.

Eseryel, U. Y., & Eseryel, D. (2013). Action-embedded transformational leadership in self-managing global information systems development teams. *Journal of Strategic Information Systems, 22*, 103–120.

Fareed, M. Z., & Su, Q. (2022). Transformational leadership and project success: A mediating role of public service motivation. *Administration & Society, 54*(4), 690–713.

Filipkowski, J., Ruth, M., & Heverin, A. (2018). *Building a coaching culture for change management*. Human Capital Institute and International Coaching Federation. https://www.hci.org/research/building-coaching-culture-change-management?check_logged_in=1. Accessed 5 June 2024.

Furnham, A., Grover, S., & McClelland, A. (2023). Choosing a coach: The influence of age, gender and experience in shaping preferences for business coaches. *Coaching: An International Journal of Theory, Research and Practice, 16*(2), 139–154.

Gartzia, L., & van Engen, M. (2012). Are (male) leaders "feminine" enough? Gendered traits of identity as mediators of sex differences in leadership styles. *Gender in Management: An International Journal, 27*(5), 296–314. https://doi.org/10.1108/17542411211252624

Gill, R. (2002). Change management—Or change leadership? *Journal of Change Management, 3*(4), 307–318.

Gill, A. S., Flaschner, A. B., & Shachar, M. (2006). Mitigating stress and burnout by implementing transformational leadership. *International Journal of Contemporary Hospitality Management, 18*(6/7), 469–481. https://doi.org/10.1108/09596110610681511

Goleman, D. (2000). Leadership that gets results. *Harvard Business Review, 78*(2), 78–90.

Goleman, D., Boyatzis, R., & McKee, A. (2002). *Primal leadership: Realizing the power of emotional intelligence*. HBR Press.

Gruman, J. A., & Saks, A. M. (2011). Performance management and employee engagement. *Human Resource Management Review, 21*(2), 123–136. https://doi.org/10.1016/j.hrmr.2010.09.004

Hamlin, R. G., Ellinger, A. D., & Beattie, R. S. (2006). Coaching at the heart of managerial effectiveness: A cross-cultural study of managerial behaviours. *Human Resource Development International, 9*(3), 305–331.

Hamlin, R. G., Patel, T., Ruiz, C., & Whitford, S. (2012). Towards a universal taxonomy of perceived managerial and leadership effectiveness: A multiple cross-case/cross-nation study of effective and ineffective managerial behaviour. In *Proceedings of the 13th UFHRD International Conference of Human Resource Development Research and Practice across Europe*. UFHRD.

Hofstede, G. (1991). *Cultures and organizations: Software of the mind*. McGraw-Hill.

Howard, A. (2006). Positive and negative emotional attractors and intentional change. *Journal of Management Development, 25*(7), 657–670.

Humphreys, J. H., & Einstein, W. O. (2003). Nothing new under the sun: Transformational leadership from a historical perspective. *Management Decision, 41*(1), 85–95.

Hunt, J. M., & Weintraub, J. (2002). How coaching can enhance your brand as a manager. *Journal of Organizational Excellence, 21*(2), 39–44. https://doi.org/10.1002/npr.10018

Hurley, R. F. (2006). The decision to trust. *Harvard Business Review, 84*(9), 55–62.

Ibarra, H., & Scoular, A. (2019). The leader as coach. *Harvard Business Review, 97*(6), 110–119.

Jackson, T. A., Meyer, J. P., & Wang, X. H. (2013). Leadership, commitment, and culture: A meta-analysis. *Journal of Leadership & Organizational Studies, 20*(1), 84–106.

Joseph, D. L., & Newman, D. A. (2010). Emotional intelligence: An integrative meta-analysis and cascading model. *Journal of Applied Psychology, 95*(1), 54.

Joo, B.-K.B. (2005). Executive coaching: A conceptual framework from an integrative review of practice and research. *Human Resource Development Review, 4*(4), 462–488.

Judge, T. A., & Piccolo, R. F. (2004). Transformational and transactional leadership: a meta-analytic test of their relative validity. *Journal of applied psychology, 89*(5), 755.

Kao, H., Craven, A. E., & Kao, T. (2006). The relationship between leadership style & demographic characteristics of Taiwanese executives. *International Business and Economics Research Journal, 5*(2), 35–48.

Kark, R., Waismel-Manor, R., & Shamir, B. (2012). Does valuing androgyny and femininity lead to a female advantage? The relationship between gender-role, transformational leadership and identification. *The Leadership Quarterly, 23*(3), 620–640.

Kalu, K. A. (2010). National culture and leadership: Followers' preference of transformational or transactional leadership in a power distance culture. In *Dissertation Abstracts International Section A: Humanities and Social Sciences, 71*(11-A), 4082.

Kim, S., Egan, T. M., Kim, W., & Kim, J. (2013). The impact of managerial coaching behavior on employee work-related reactions. *Journal of Business and Psychology, 28*, 315–330.

Kim, S., Egan, T. M., & Moon, M. J. (2014). Managerial coaching efficacy, work-related attitudes, and performance in public organizations: A comparative international study. *Review of Public Personnel Administration, 34*(3), 237–262.

Ladyshewsky, R. K. (2010). The manager as coach as a driver of organizational development. *Leadership & Organization Development Journal, 31*(4), 292–306.

Martin, J. (2015). Transformational and transactional leadership: An exploration of gender, experience, and institution type. *Portal: Libraries and the Academy, 15*(2), 331–351.

Martinez, S. A., & Leija, N. (2023). Distinguishing servant leadership from transactional and transformational leadership. *Advances in Developing Human Resources, 25*(3), 141–188.

Maslow, A. (1970). *Motivation and personality* (2nd ed.). Harper and Row.

Oke, A., Walumbwa, F. O., & Myers, A. (2012). Innovation strategy, human resource policy, and firms' revenue growth: The roles of environmental uncertainty and innovation performance. *Decision Sciences, 43*(2), 273–302. https://doi.org/10.1111/j.1540-5915.2011.00350.x

Patel, T., Hamlin, R. G., & Louis, D. (2022). Toward a generic framework of negative manager/leader behavior: A comparative study across nations and private sector industries. *European Management Review*, 1–17, https://doi.org/10.1111/emre.12507

Potosky, D., & Azan, W. (2023). Leadership behaviors and human agency in the valley of despair: A meta-framework for organizational change implementation. *Human Resource Management Review, 33*, 100927. https://doi.org/10.1016/j.hrmr.2022.100927

Powell, G. N., Butterfield, D. A., Alves, J. C., & Bartol, K. M. (2004). Sex effects in evaluations of transformational and transactional leaders. *Academy of Management Proceedings, 2004*(1), E1–E6. Academy of Management.

Rafferty, A. E., & Griffin, M. A. (2004). Dimensions of transformational leadership: Conceptual and empirical extensions. *The leadership quarterly, 15*(3), 329–354.

Rhee, K. S., & Sigler, T. H. (2015). Untangling the relationship between gender and leadership. *Gender in Management: An International Journal, 30*(2), 109–134. https://doi.org/10.1108/GM-09-2013-0114

Robison, J. (2020, January 17). *Give up bossing, take up coaching: You'll like the results.* https://www.gallup.com/workplace/282647/give-bossing-coaching-results.aspx. Accessed 29 July 2024.

Rockstuhl, T., Wu, D., Dulebohn, J. H., Liao, C., & Hoch, J. E. (2023). Cultural congruence or compensation? A meta-analytic test of transformational and transactional leadership effects across cultures. *Journal of International Business Studies, 54*(3), 476–504.

Schaufeli, W., & Salanova, M. (2007). Work engagement: An emerging psychological concept and its implications for organizations. In S. W. Gilliland, D. D. Steiner, & D. P. Skarlicki (Eds.), *Managing Social and Ethical Issues in Organizations* (pp. 135–177). Information Age Publishing.

Šiber, A. B., Erceg, N., Rebrina, M., & Galić, Z. (2023). Gender differences in managerial effectiveness and the role of transformational leadership and intellectual humility. *Psihologijske teme, 32*(3), 597–613. https://doi.org/10.31820/pt.32.3.10

Sonthalia, S. (2024). Evaluating the impact of embodying the coaching mindset on leaders' paradigm of power. *Coaching: An International Journal of*

Theory, Research and Practice, 17(2), 248–264. https://doi.org/10.1080/17521882.2024.2312282

Shahin, A. I., & Wright, P. L. (2004). Leadership in the context of culture: An Egyptian perspective. *Leadership & Organization Development Journal, 25*(5/6), 499–511. https://doi.org/10.1108/01437730410556743

Simola, S. K., Barling, J., & Turner, N. (2010). Transformational leadership and leader moral orientation: Contrasting an ethic of justice and an ethic of care. *The Leadership Quarterly, 21*(1), 179–188. https://doi.org/10.1016/j.leaqua.2009.10.013

Singh, H., Singh, S. K., & Singh, L. (2022). A study on the effectiveness of transactional and transformational styles of leadership. *International Journal of Management, Public Policy and Research, 1*(2), 6–11. https://doi.org/10.55829/010202

Stone, A. G., Russell, R. F., & Patterson, K. (2004). Transformational versus servant leadership: A difference in leader focus. *Leadership & Organization Development Journal, 25*(4), 349–361.

Stout-Rostron, S., Passmore, J., Peterson, D., & Freire, T. (2013). Gender issues in business coaching. In J. Passmore, D. B. Peterson, & T. Freire (Eds.), *The Wiley-Blackwell Handbook of the Psychology of Coaching and Mentoring* (pp. 155–174). John Wiley & Sons Ltd.

Taylor, S. N. (2010). Redefining leader self-awareness by integrating the second component of self-awareness. *Journal of Leadership Studies, 3*(4), 57–68. https://doi.org/10.1002/jls.20139

Tyler, J. A. (2011). Reclaiming rare listening as a means of organizational re-enchantment. *Journal of Organizational Change Management, 24*(1), 143–157.

van Engen, M. L., & Willemsen, T. M. (2004). Sex and leadership styles: A meta-analysis of research published in the 1990s. *Psychological Reports, 94*(1), 3–18.

Walumbwa, F. O., Orwa, B., Wang, P., & Lawler, J. J. (2005). Transformational leadership, organizational commitment, and job satisfaction: A comparative study of Kenya and the U.S. finance firms. *Human Resource Development Quarterly, 16*(2), 235–256.

Wang, X. H. F., & Howell, J. M. (2012). A multilevel study of transformational leadership, identification, and follower outcomes. *The Leadership Quarterly, 23*(5), 775–790.

Wang, G., Oh, I. S., Courtright, S. H., & Colbert, A. E. (2011). Transformational leadership and performance across criteria and levels: A meta-analytic review of 25 years of research. *Group & Organization Management, 36*(2), 223–270.

Wasylysyn, K. (2003). Executive coaching: An outcome study. *Consulting Psychology Journal Practice and Research, 55*(2), 94–106.

Widodo, W., & Mawarto, M. (2020). Investigating the role of innovative behavior in mediating the effect of transformational leadership and talent management on performance. *Management Science Letters, 10*(10), 2175–2182.

Wilson, C. (2007). *Best practice in performance coaching: A handbook for leaders, coaches, HR professionals and organizations.* Kogan Page.

Xanthopoulou, D., Bakker, A. B., Demerouti, E., & Schaufeli, W. B. (2009). Reciprocal relationships between job resources, personal resources, and work engagement. *Journal of Vocational Behavior, 74*(3), 235–244.

Ye, R., Wang, X. H., Wendt, J. H., Wu, J., & Euwema, M. C. (2016). Gender and managerial coaching across cultures: Female managers are coaching more. *The International Journal of Human Resource Management, 27*(16), 1791–1812. https://doi.org/10.1080/09585192.2015.1075570

Yukl, G. (2013). *Leadership in organizations* (8th ed.). Pearson.

Zheng, L., Wang, Y., Guo, Z., & Zhu, Y. (2022). Effects of managerial coaching on employees' creative performance: Cross-level moderating role of a climate for innovation. *Leadership & Organization Development Journal, 43*(2), 211–224. https://doi.org/10.1108/LODJ-03-2021-0132

Zhu, W., Avolio, B. J., & Walumbwa, F. O. (2009). Moderating role of follower characteristics with transformational leadership and follower work engagement. *Group & Organization Management, 34*, 590–619. https://doi.org/10.1177/1059601108331242

Żukowska, J., & Miąsek, D. (2014). The role of coaching in managerial careers of women. *Women & Business*, 1–4.

CHAPTER 9

Super Empathetic Compassionate Servant Leaders

Abstract This chapter describes the leader with super empathy who leads with compassion. Other descriptors of this type of leader include servant leaders, authentic leaders, compassionate leaders, and resonant leaders. The distinguishing characteristic of this type of leader is that they put their follower first, before the organization, unlike all other leaders. This is because of their super empathy. Servant leaders increase work engagement, self-efficacy, OCB, job attitudes, and performance of their subordinates.

Keywords Super empathy · Servant leader · Compassionate leader · Authentic leader · Resonant leader

At this end of the spectrum is the leader who is totally empathetic, and who is able to ascertain the needs of their direct report and be the perfect coach that they need. This leader is free of ego, free of having to direct their subordinate to meet their own needs but has the best interests of their subordinate in mind. This leader is compassionate, is a servant leader, is mindful, is resonant, is authentic, and wise. From a Maslow point of view, they would be completely self-actualized. There are examples of these kinds of leaders, and they are rare. However, this is the type of leader that leaders with a coaching mindset could aspire to be. Some

B. W. Eversole, *The Leadership Spectrum*, https://doi.org/10.1007/978-3-031-73557-8_9

leaders are naturally empathetic. While there are no genes for empathy, there is a genetic predisposition, which when combined with environmental triggers, results in empathy (Baron-Cohen, 2011). Yet empathy is also a skill that can be learned (Gerdes et al., 2011) and developed (Kaplan et al., 1991).

The purpose of this book is to provide a road map toward increasing empathy in leaders. At this point it is important to note that total empathy is necessary but not sufficient to be this type of leader. Empathetic leaders who lead with empathy still need to excel in the technical tasks of supervision/management/leadership in order to be great leaders.

Leaders at this level would have what Baron-Cohen (2011) calls super empathy or Level 6; they are at the high end of the empathy curve and have over-activity of the empathy circuit. They not only feel the emotions of others but are able to separate those feelings from their own, so that they are not distressed by them. There are many types of leaders described in the literature that we can put at this end of the spectrum. The most popular is the concept of the servant leader.

SERVANT LEADERS

Robert Greenleaf coined the term servant leadership:

> The Servant-Leader is servant first... It begins with the natural feeling that one wants to serve, to serve first. Then conscious choice brings one to aspire to lead...The best test, and difficult to administer is this: Do those served grow as persons? Do they, while being served, become healthier, wiser, freer, more autonomous, and more likely themselves to become servants? And, what is the effect on the least privileged in society? Will they benefit, or at least not further be harmed? (Greenleaf, 1977, p. 7)
> This definition of servant leaders has been refined and updated by Eva et al. (2019):
> Servant leadership is an (1) other-oriented approach to leadership (2) manifested through one-on-one prioritizing of follower individual needs and interests, (3) and outward reorienting of their concern for self towards concern for others within the organization and the larger community. (p. 114).

As servant leaders are motivated by the need to serve, they are not motivated by the need for power like other leaders (Luthans & Avolio, 2003).

Traits

Servant leaders have a great deal of empathy for their direct reports (Barbuto et al. 2014; Bragger et al., 2021; Liden et al., 2014; Martinez & Leija, 2023; Spears & Lawrence, 2002). They also have these additional characteristics: (van Dierendonck, 2011): they are humble and authentic; they empower and develop people; they are caretakers who supply recommendations for others for the benefit of the entire enterprise; and they are accepting of others for who they really are. Instead of expecting others to serve them, servant leaders serve their followers; servant leaders are concerned with their development and growth. In order to serve others, servant leaders must have a high level of emotional intelligence as well as empathy to understand others' feelings and put them above their own (Liden et al., 2014). It is important to note that for servant leaders, the inclination to serve is secondary to the inclination to lead (Daft & Lengel, 2000).

Behaviors

Servant leaders can be thought of as having not only attributes but also behaviors (Sendjaya et al., 2008). Empathy is an attribute of a servant leader that is observed by their showing consideration, care, understanding, or other empathetic feedback, or by actively listening (Martinez & Leija, 2023). Servant leadership is not only what one does (doing service), but also who one is (being a servant) (Sendjaya & Sarros, 2002).

Outcomes

Servant leaders increase their subordinates' work engagement (de Clercq et al., 2014) and their self-efficacy (Wu et al., 2021), as well as performance, attitudes, and citizenship behavior (Liden et al., 2014; van Dierendonck, 2011). Research has demonstrated that servant leadership is related to follower outcomes, including job attitudes, organizational citizenship behavior (OCB), and performance (Liden et al., 2014; van Dierendonck, 2011). As Lemoine and Blum (2021) note, "this style of leadership emerges as a holistic theory of effective management, boosting performance while prioritizing a range of positive outcomes" (p. 23). Servant leaders can improve the resilience of their followers (Eliot, 2020).

Most leaders who have been considered great historically, have put their followers first (Spain, 2019).

Compassionate Leaders

To understand compassionate leaders, we need to delve a little further into the concept of empathy, which can be thought of as a concept with many facets (Decety, 2010). Scholars differ on the definition of compassion or concern. Goleman (2006) and Baron-Cohen (2011) consider empathy to include action in a compassionate way, while Hougaard and Carter (2022) define compassion as empathy plus action. Jordan et al. (2016) separate compassion from affective empathy using the concept of empathic concern, which does not share the emotional experience of another. Lilius et al. (2008) defined compassion as "… noticing another person's suffering, empathically feeling another person's pain, and acting in a manner to ease the suffering" (pp. 94–95). Kornfield defined it as "the heart's response to sorrow" (p. 326). No matter how we define empathy, compassion, and their relationship to each other, it is clear that both are present in the compassionate leader.

There isn't much research about compassionate leaders (Krause et al., 2023a; Shuck et al. 2019). According to Shuck et al. (2019) compassionate leader behavior is distinct from servant leader or authentic leader behaviors; however, Krause et al. (2023b) found that compassionate leader behaviors covaried with servant leadership. Compassionate leaders react to the suffering of their subordinates (Kanov et al., 2004; Lilius et al., 2008). They connect with empathy and then lead with compassion (Hougaard & Carter, 2022). Shuck et al. (2019) found six building blocks of compassionate leader behavior: "integrity, empathy, accountability, authenticity, presence, and dignity" (p. 538). Krause et al. (2023a) found six paradoxes that leaders need to deal with when being compassionate with their direct reports: (1) their subordinates' struggle to show their suffering while still wanting to be professional; (2) leaders wanting to respect boundaries yet needing to ask questions to understand the suffering; (3) leaders wanting to show compassion yet needing to be careful not to be manipulated or exploited; (4) the difficulty of showing compassion for one subordinate's suffering and still being fair to other direct reports; (5) the concern that others in their organization will view their compassion as a sign of weakness rather than courage; and (6) the difficulty of maintaining the hierarchical relationship with a direct report while being compassionate with them (p. 5).

Compassionate leaders are also wise and mindful (Hougaard & Carter, 2022). Sutton (2012) described wise bosses who were empathetic and compassionate. They gain empathy for their direct reports by listening, helping, and learning from them. Sutton relayed his own personal experience of a wise boss who helped him through a crisis with his son by enabling him to work remotely a few days a week. Wise bosses also display appreciation and gratitude. Carroll (2008) described mindful leaders who practice what the Tibetans call "jinpa" (pp. 24–25). Practicing jinpa means to be undefended, engaged, and vulnerable, and to authentically listen to an unhappy direct report. The practice of mindfulness increases both compassion and wisdom (Hougaard & Carter, 2022).

Compassionate leaders are also caring (Hougaard & Carter, 2022), as they have all the qualities of civil, effective/caring, and coaching leaders. Hougaard and Carter (2022) modeled the Wise Compassion Flywheel (p. 105) which includes "Caring Presence (be here now), Caring Courage (courage over comfort), Caring candor (direct is faster), and Caring transparency (clarity is kindness)," which should be practiced by all compassionate leaders.

Compassionate leaders can create healthy organizational cultures and improve learning, as well as improving civility and decreasing conflict in organizations (Shuck et al. 2019). Krause et al. (2023b) found that compassionate leader behaviors had a positive association with psychological safety. Psychological safety means that direct reports can voice concerns and ideas without fear of retribution (Edmondson, 1999).

AUTHENTIC LEADERS

Authentic leadership is a "pattern of leader behavior that draws upon and promotes both positive psychological capacities and a positive ethical climate, to foster greater self-awareness, an internalized moral perspective, balanced processing of information, and relational transparency on the part of leaders working with followers, fostering positive self-development" (Walumbwa et al., 2008, p. 94). Acting in a way that is congruent with their own self-concept is necessary to being authentic, to being able to share their feelings and demonstrate their true care and compassion (Atwijuka & Caldwell, 2017). Servant leaders are also authentic leaders (Avolio & Gardner, 2005). Both servant leaders and authentic leaders focus on the development of their followers but are also aware of the importance of self-regulation for authentic behavior and self-awareness. Authentic leaders are positive and are deeply aware of both their own and others' perspectives (Avolio et al., 2004; Gardner et al., 2005).

RESONANT LEADERS

Goleman et al. (2002) described primal, resonant leaders, leaders who handle their relationships with their competence in emotional intelligence. Their high emotional intelligence helps them to drive the emotions of who they lead in the right direction. A resonant leader (Goleman et al., 2002) has empathy and can read the emotions of others, resonating with them. They are also authentic leaders and leave people uplifted and inspired.

As Goleman et al. (2002) notes, "One sign of resonant leadership is a group of followers who vibrate with a leader's upbeat and enthusiastic energy" (p.20). When followers are upset or angry about something, the resonant leader, with high EI and empathy, also has resonance for those emotions as well, and expresses them too for the group. This leaves direct reports feeling cared for and understood. Work feels more meaningful, and the team bonds at an emotional level.

ADAPTIVE LEADERS

Heifetz et al. (2009) described adaptive leadership as a type of leadership that focused on followers, helping them to thrive in particularly challenging and difficult situations requiring flexibility and change. "The core function of adaptive leaders is about helping others to explore, to change and to learn new behaviors to effectively meet their challenges and grow in the adaptive process (Meng et al., 2024, p. 505)." Adaptive leaders change how their followers work together, rather than changing what they do (Kuluski et al., 2021).

Emotional intelligence, and especially empathy, is perhaps the most important characteristic for an adaptive leader (Ferris, 2019; Henman, n.d.; Yukl & Mahsud 2010). Moreover, adaptive leaders need to foster an inclusive culture of psychological safety, mutual trust, and candor (Ramalingam et al., 2022). Adaptive leaders work with their followers using six strategies, two of which require empathy: alignment conversations and interpreting (Kuluski et al., 2021). Alignment conversations involve discovering why followers are resisting change and being empathetic and compassionate while discussing their concerns and their fear about the changes. Being interpretive means being empathetic and reading followers' non-verbal facial expressions, body language, and silence. Heifetz et al. (2009) called this "listening for the song beneath the words (p. 22)."

RELATED DESCRIPTIONS

Wood et al. (2021) introduced the notion of the integral leader. These leaders are humanistic, self-aware, and also situationally aware. They are also trustworthy, competent, and inclusive. While the authors did not mention empathy, they mentioned many emotional intelligence traits close to empathy in their model. The integral leader can only be achieved with psychological training, i.e., they need to understand the notion of leadership as including both bad and good elements and have the emotional regulation to control their own bad tendencies (Wood & Petriglieri, 2005).

The transcendent leader (note "transcendence" as the highest motive in Maslow's (1970) hierarchy) has transcendent motives which are the "desire to bring about a certain outcome not in the agent who acts, but in the other" (Argandoña, 2011, p. 79). These motives relate to service to the needs of others.

Wickman (2021) described an evolved leader with four traits: they are caring, act with candor, build connection, and change. This caring leader creates psychological safety for their team. Employees also need to feel like they can depend on their leader. As Wickman (2021) put it, "This sense of care requires a deep ability to listen, to practice empathy, to manage one's emotions, and to be able to sense and respond to the emotional conditions present for the team" (p. 55). The evolved leader also demonstrates candor that is clear and kind when giving feedback to employees and makes sure that their emotional state matches the feedback that is given. Evolved leaders also are attuned to the emotional needs of their employees and respond to them in a way that makes them feel that they are there for them. Employees will feel a sense of connection when leaders are encouraging and available to them.

Csikszentmihalyi (2004) in his book *Good Business*, describes what "sets a visionary leader apart, however, is their unbounded optimism and trust in fellow humans, and their veneration for empathy and respect" (p. 165). He goes on to say that these leaders sincerely believe that they are working to make a better world, that "their message appeals to the soul, to the need we all have to connect with a greater purpose, that others are willing to follow their lead and find flow in their work" (p. 165).

Compassionate servant leaders can also be considered decent (Harrison, 2007). Decent managers utilize appreciation, dignity, genuine care, and empathy in their relationships with their employees according to Hadžiomerović et al. (2021). McNamee (2018) went further: "decency... carries an element of soulcraft to it: it goes deeper, into character more than manners" (p. 224), concerning itself with what is right and wrong; what is moral and ethical. According to Boulding (2019), a leader's Decency Quotient (DQ) should be just as important as their IQ and EQ (Emotional Quotient, from Emotional Intelligence). It is not enough to just have empathy, but leaders need to show care for their employees as well. Moreover, like servant leadership, decent leaders may put the organization second to their followers (Hadžiomerović et al., 2021).

Exemplars of Super Empathetic Leaders

At the most fundamental level, it is an honor to serve—at whatever type of size of an organization you are privileged to lead, whether it is a for-profit or non-profit.—Alan Mulally

Alan Mulally, former CEO of Ford, was a servant leader who believes it is an honor to serve his organization (DiPietropolo, 2021). Tricia Griffith, CEO of Progressive Insurance, is also known for her servant leadership style (ceo-na.com, 2024). Her leadership style of "leading with her heart" has increased Progressive's stock price 4X over six years (Morgan, 2022). Herb Kelleher of Southwest Airlines was a servant leader (leadx.org, n.d.). He put his employees first, and told his managers to be tough but not mean, because being mean (dehumanizing, belittling, shaming) would get them fired (Freiburg & Freiburg, 2019). Cheryl Bachelder, former CEO of Popeyes, was a servant leader (Miller, 2022). Servant leadership helped her turn the company around to profitability from bankruptcy in a few years. Art Barter, owner of Datron World Communications, was a servant leader who grew his company from $10 to $200 million in six years (Servant Leadership Institute, n.d.) Alan Jope, former CEO of

Unilever, had this to say about compassionate and wise leadership: "All business sectors care about business performance. This book [Hougaard and Carter's (2022) *Compassionate leadership*] uses deep research to demonstrate that compassionate and wise leadership is not an alternative to a performance culture, but is a key accelerant of it" (Amazon.com, n.d.) However, focusing on a sustainability and environmental strategy cost Jope his position, and he was forced to take early retirement in 2023 (Lyubomirova, 2023). Being a compassionate leader is not without its risks.

I know a Chair of a large organization who had an underperforming CEO who was behaving badly working for them. One of their board members advised them to "take the CEO out to the woodshed." The Chair declined this advice, preferring to work with the Board to develop a dignified exit package. Meanwhile, my friend gave the CEO constructive feedback and let them figure out on their own that things were not working out. The CEO ended up resigning, and the Chair worked hard to find a new replacement who was fully supported by the Board, and then the Chair worked tirelessly to onboard the new CEO. The old CEO was able to leave their position in a humane, dignified way. When I asked the Chair why they worked so hard to let the CEO leave in a humane and dignified way even though they had acted badly, they said, "everyone deserves to be treated that way."

Illinois governor J.B. Pritzker gave a commencement speech in 2023 at Northwestern University on how to "spot an idiot" based on their lack of kindness and empathy. He noted:

> The best way to spot an idiot, look for the person who is cruel. Let me explain. When we see someone who doesn't look like us, or sound like us, or love like us, or live like us, the first thought that crosses almost everyone's brain is rooted in either fear or judgement or both. That's evolution. We survived as a species by being suspicious of things that we aren't familiar with. In order to be kind, we have to shut down that animal instinct and force our brain to travel a different pathway. Empathy and compassion are evolved states of being. They require the mental capacity to step past our most primal urges. This may be a surprising assessment because somewhere along the way in the last few years, our society has come to believe that weaponized cruelty is part of some well-thought-out Master plan. Cruelty is seen by some as an adroit cudgel to gain power. Empathy and kindness are considered weak. Many important people look at the vulnerable only as rungs on a ladder to the top. I'm here to tell

you that when someone's path through this world is marked with acts of cruelty, they have failed the first test of an advanced society. They never forced their animal brain to evolve past its first instinct. They never forged new mental pathways to overcome their own instinctual fears. And so, their thinking and problem solving will lack the imagination and creativity that the kindest people have in spades. Over my many years in politics and business I have found one thing to be universally true. The kindest person in the room is often the smartest (Pritzker, 2023).

My Chair friend was the kindest person in the room.

GENDER AND SUPER EMPATHETIC LEADERS

Servant leadership has the potential to unlock leadership opportunities for women to lead effectively while maintaining a feminine style, empowering women leaders to inhabit both leader and gender roles authentically. (Lehrke & Sowden, 2017, p. 26)

Women servant leaders obtain higher performance from followers than men, possibly due to role congruity (Lemoine & Blum, 2021). In fact, social role theory may predict that women are more drawn to a servant leadership style (Duff, 2013). In a small study by Hogue (2016), participants expected servant leader behaviors more from woman leaders than from men. Today's workforce, comprised of Millennials and Gen Z, wants leaders who engage, transform, and inspire them (McCollum, 2024). "This paradigm shift calls for the gifts that have been reinforced in women throughout their lives—characteristics such as empathy, vulnerability, authenticity, and inclusion. When we scour our leadership database informed by 360-degree assessments and study gender differences in inclusive leadership behaviors, raters rank women as significantly better" (p. 20). Politis and Politis (2018) studied servant leaders in Cyprus and found that women servant leaders had a negative influence on managerial misconduct, while men servant leaders had the opposite effect. Women scored slightly higher than men on a Compassion instrument, showing a stronger focus on compassion (Depow et al., 2023) and are rated more compassionate than men (Hougaard & Carter, 2022). Women with feminine traits may be better suited as evolved leaders (Wickman, 2021).

Culture and Super Empathetic Leaders

Plank and Reid (2010) speculated that empathy may be less important in countries with higher power distances. Yet Rahman (2016) of Malaysia, a high power distance country, noted that globalization requires that companies improve the empathy skills of their employees in order to survive. In fact, empathy is important for leaders during global expansion or relocation, due to their adaptability and openness to new environments (Goleman, 2006; Mahsud et al., 2010). In Nabih et al.'s (2023) study in Egypt, emotional intelligence was positively related to leader effectiveness. Rodriguez-Rubio and Kiser (2013) did a study in Mexico comparing that country with the U.S. and found that women in both of those countries were more likely than men to have values that are congruent with servant leaders, such as service to others.

Conclusion

We've noted several times in this book that empathy is not enough; a leader still has to be competent in order to be successful. Sutton (2012) notes that great bosses still need to drive performance. He noted that "Bosses who are civilized and caring but incompetent, can be horrible" (p. 266). Empathy is necessary but not sufficient for great bosses. It's especially important when it comes to performance reviews. Scott (2019) calls this "ruinous empathy": caring too much about your people's feelings that you do not challenge them when necessary. Your subordinates need honest feedback, those who are performing at a high level are demotivated if everyone gets the same rating, and not doing your job means someone else has to do it. This chapter has focused on the ingredient that bosses have to get right in their relationship with their direct reports in order to be great leaders: they must have empathy and compassion for them. We now turn to the last chapter in the book, where we discuss how we might help bad leaders turn into good ones. We will start with the leaders in the center of the spectrum, the uncivil leaders, for two reasons. First, they are the most common type of bad leader. Second, since they are only mildly abusive, and perhaps unintentionally so, they should be the easiest to develop into better leaders. In this way, we could get the biggest bang for our developmental buck, helping the most subordinates live better work lives.

REFERENCES

Amazon.com. (n.d.). Book review. https://www.amazon.com/Compassio
nate-Leadership-Hard-Things-Human/dp/1647820731/ref=sr_1_1?crid=
SPALDBWF5Z44&dib=eyJ2IjoiMSJ9.fYeDTA8SkPdmlFndigXS-TVCYea
eT9EVNXGBhYWFTTX8KbTspgWAOucj_d0k5QQrNxUbOo6pOg4Q_p
BCvZ2S8dAj0jnHQTO_PeeU1COMh3obpkbVjJHceBDcyFLc-aBwaA0td2
E92Ud_rOjtgcLojAePQeIHvhs_n5Ezcfy4pBLxa9YdQPYRW5Dq6DKGUgU
S9pOryQN795L4ady7SehYtTij9xegZ_kqCx8tVzjTYHE.x49A34KoypofEuN
jOKq6YlgoN2M-oxNKNy-iw7gZqdY&dib_tag=se&keywords=Compassio
nate+Leadership&qid=1722283687&s=books&sprefix=compassionate+leader
ship%2Cstripbooks%2C138&sr=1-1. Accessed 29 July 2024.
Argandoña, A. (2011). Beyond contracts: Love in firms. *Journal of Business Ethics, 99*, 77–85. https://doi.org/10.1007/si0551-01
Atwijuka, S., & Caldwell, C. (2017). Authentic leadership and the ethic of care. *Journal of Management Development, 36*(8), 1040–1051.
Avolio, B. J., & Gardner, W. L. (2005). Authentic leadership development: Getting to the root of positive forms of leadership. *The Leadership Quarterly, 16*(3), 315–338.
Avolio, B. J., Zhu, W., Koh, W., & Bhatia, P. (2004). Transformational leadership and organizational commitment: Mediating role of psychological empowerment and moderating role of structural distance. *Journal of Organizational Behavior, 25*(8), 951–968. https://doi.org/10.1002/job.283
Barbuto Jr, J. E., Gottfredson, R. K., & Searle, T. P. (2014). An examination of emotional intelligence as an antecedent of servant leadership. *Journal of Leadership & Organizational Studies, 21*(3), 315–323.
Baron-Cohen, S. (2011). *The science of evil: On empathy and the origins of cruelty.* Basic Books.
Bragger, J. D., Alonso, N. A., D'Ambrosio, K., & Williams, N. (2021). Developing leaders to serve and servants to lead. *Human Resource Development Review, 20*(1), 9–45.
Boulding, B. (2019, July 16). For leaders, decency is just as important as intelligence. *Harvard Business Review.* https://hbr.org/2019/07/for-leaders-dec ency-is-just-as-important-as-intelligence. Accessed 9 June 2024.
Carroll, M. (2008). *The mindful leader: Awakening your natural management skills through mindfulness meditation.* Shambhala Publications.
Ceo-na.com. (2024, July 29). Progressive CEO: Tricia Griffith. CEO North America. https://ceo-na.com/executive-interviews/a-progressive-bus iness-woman/. Accessed 29 July 2024.
Csikszentmihalyi, M. (2004). *Good business: Leadership, flow, and the making of meaning.* Penguin.
Daft, R. L., & Lengel, R. H. (2000). *Fusion leadership: Unlocking the subtle forces that change people and organizations.* Berrett-Koehler.

Decety, J. (2010). The neurodevelopment of empathy in humans. *Developmental Neuroscience, 32*(4), 257–267. https://doi.org/10.1159/000317771

de Clercq, D., Bouckenooghe, D., Raja, U., & Matsyborska, G. (2014). Servant leadership and work engagement: The contingency effects of leader-follower social capital. *Human Resource Development Quarterly, 25*(2), 183–212.

Depow, G. J., Hobson, N. M., Beck, J., Inzlicht, M., & Hougaard, R. (2023, June 1). The compassion advantage: Leaders who care outperform leaders who share followers' emotions. https://doi.org/10.31234/osf.io/md2g8

DiPietropolo, C. (2021, February 17). Leadership: What can we learn from Alan Mulally and Ford Motor Company? Part 1. https://www.leaderessentialsgroup.com/post/leadership-what-can-we-learn-from-allan-mullaly-and-ford-motor-company-part-1. Accessed 29 July 2024.

Duff, A. J. (2013). Performance management coaching: Servant leadership and gender implications. *Leadership & Organization Development Journal, 34*(3), 204–221. https://doi.org/10.1108/01437731311326657

Edmondson, A. (1999). Psychological safety and learning behavior in work teams. *Administrative Science Quarterly, 44*(2), 350–383.

Eliot, J. L. (2020). Resilient leadership: The impact of a servant leader on the resilience of their followers. *Advances in Developing Human Resources, 22*(4), 404–418. https://doi.org/10.1177/1523422320945237

Eva, N., Robin, M., Sendjaya, S., Van Dierendonck, D., & Liden, R. C. (2019). Servant leadership: A systematic review and call for future research. *The Leadership Quarterly, 30*(1), 111–132. https://doi.org/10.1016/j.leaqua.2018.07.004

Ferris, K. (2019, October 9).Adaptive leadership—Empathy and empowerment. https://www.thedigitaltransformationpeople.com/channels/people-and-change/adaptive-leadership-empathy-and-empowerment/. Accessed 2 November 2024.

Freiburg, K., & Freiburg, J. (2019, April 7). 20 reasons why Herb Kelleher was one of the most beloved leaders of our time. *Forbes.* https://www.forbes.com/sites/kevinandjackiefreiberg/2019/01/04/20-reasons-why-herb-kelleher-was-one-of-the-most-beloved-leaders-of-our-time/?sh=73f0cb0cb311. Accessed 29 July 2024.

Gardner, W. L., Avolio, B. J., Luthans, F., May, D. R., & Walumbwa, F. (2005). "Can you see the real me?" A self-based model of authentic leader and follower development. *The Leadership Quarterly, 16*(3), 343–372. https://doi.org/10.1016/j.leaqua.2005.03.003

Gerdes, K. E., Segal, E. A., Jackson, K. F., & Mullins, J. L. (2011). Teaching empathy: A framework rooted in social cognitive neuroscience and social justice. *Journal of Social Work Education, 47*(1), 109–131.

Goleman, D. (2006). *Social intelligence: The new science of human relationships.* Bantam Books.

Goleman, D., Boyatzis, R., McKee, A., & Patterson, S. (2002). *Primal leadership: Realizing the power of emotional intelligence.* Harvard Business School Press.

Greenleaf, R. K. (1977). *Servant leadership: A journey into the nature of legitimate power and greatness.* Paulist Press.

Hadžiomerović, B., Kurtić, E., & Arslanagić Kalajdžić, M. (2021). Understanding the dimensions of managerial decency construct. *Management: Journal of Contemporary Management Issues, 26*(1), 37–62. https://doi.org/10.30924/mjcmi.26.1.4

Harrison, S. G. (2007). *The manager's book of decencies: How small gestures build great companies.* McGraw Hill Professional.

Heifetz, R., Grashow, A., & Linsky, M. (2009). The theory behind the practice: A brief introduction to the adaptive leadership framework. In *The practice of adaptive leadership: Tools and tactics for changing your organization and the world* (pp. 1–34). Harvard Business Press.

Hogue, M. (2016). Gender bias in communal leadership: Examining servant leadership. *Journal of Managerial Psychology, 31*(4), 837–849. https://doi.org/10.1108/JMP-10-2014-0292

Hougaard, R., & Carter, J. (2022). *Compassionate leadership: How to do hard things in a human way.* Harvard Business Press.

Jordan, M. R., Amir, D., & Bloom, P. (2016). Are empathy and concern psychologically distinct? *Emotion, 16*(8), 1107–1116. https://doi.org/10.1037/2Femo0000228

Kanov, J. M., Maitlis, S., Worline, M. C., Dutton, J. E., Frost, P. J., & Lilius, J. M. (2004). Compassion in organizational life. *American Behavioral Scientist, 47*(6), 808–827.

Kaplan, R. E., Drath, W. H. & Kofodimos, J. R. (1991). *Beyond ambition: How driven managers can lead better and live better.* Jossey-Bass.

Krause, V., Rousset, C., & Schäfer, B. (2023a). Uncovering paradoxes of compassion at work: A dyadic study of compassionate leader behavior. *Frontiers in Psychology, 14*, 1112644. https://doi.org/10.3389/fpsyg.2023.1112644

Krause, V., Rousset, C., & Steinmueller, I. (2023b). Breaking the silence: Unveiling the power of compassionate leadership on employee silence. *Emerging Technologies and Future of Work, 117*, 260–269. https://doi.org/10.54941/ahfe1004426

Kuluski, K., Reid, R. J., & Baker, G. R. (2021). Applying the principles of adaptive leadership to person-centered care for people with complex care needs: Considerations for care providers, patients, caregivers and organizations. *Health Expectations: An International Journal of Public Participation in Health Care and Health Policy, 24*(2), 175–181.

Leadx.org. (n.d.). Servant leadership: Definition, examples, characteristics. https://leadx.org/articles/servant-leadership-definition-examples-characteristics/. Accessed 29 July 2024.

Lehrke, A. S., & Sowden, K. (2017). Servant leadership and gender. In C. J. Davis (Ed.), *Servant leadership and followership: Examining the impact on workplace behavior* (pp. 25–50). Palgrave MacMillan.

Lemoine, G. J., & Blum, T. C. (2021). Servant leadership, leader gender, and team gender role: Testing a female advantage in a cascading model of performance. *Personnel Psychology, 74*(1), 3–28.

Liden, R. C., Wayne, S. J., Liao, C., & Meuser, J. D. (2014). Servant leadership and serving culture: Influence on individual and unit performance. *Academy of Management Journal, 57*(5), 1434–1452. https://doi.org/10.5465/amj.2013.0034

Lilius, J. M., Kanov, J., Dutton, J. E., Worline, M. C., & Maitlis, S. (2012). Compassion revealed: What we know about compassion at work (and where we need to know more). In G. M. Spreitzer & K. S. Cameron (Eds.) *The Oxford handbook of positive organizational scholarship* (pp. 273–287). Oxford Academic Press. https://doi.org/10.1093/oxfordhb/9780199734610.013.0021

Luthans, F., & Avolio, B. (2003). Authentic leadership development. In K. S. Cameron & J. E. Dutton. (Eds.) *Positive organizational scholarship* (pp. 241–254). Berrett-Koehler.

Lyubomirova, T. (2023, January 30). FrieslandCampina CEO to replace Alan Jope at Unilever. https://www.dairyreporter.com/Article/2023/01/30/FrieslandCampina-s-Hein-Schumacher-to-replace-Alan-Jope-at-Unilever/. Accessed Jan. 9, 2025.

Mahsud, R., Yukl, G., & Prussia, G. (2010). Leader empathy, ethical relationship, and relations-oriented behaviors as antecedents of leader-member exchange quality. *Journal of Managerial Psychology, 25*(6), 561–577.

Martinez, S. A., & Leija, N. (2023). Distinguishing servant leadership from transactional and transformational leadership. *Advances in Developing Human Resources, 25*(3), 141–188.

McCollum, J. (2024). Why the leadership gender gap matters—And what organizations can do to close it. *Leader to Leader, 2024*(112), 19–25.

McNamee, G. (2018). Civility vs. Decency. *The Virginia Quarterly Review, 94*(3), 224–227.

Meng, J., Pan, P.-L., Cacciatore, M. A., & Sanchez, K. R. (2024). The integrated role of adaptive leadership, sense of empathy and communication transparency: Trust building in corporate communication during the pandemic. *Corporate Communications: An International Journal, 29*(4), 503–515.

Miller, H. L. (2022, May 11). Former CEO of Popeyes used servant leadership to save the company. *Leaders.* https://leaders.com/articles/leaders-stories/cheryl-bachelder/. Accessed 29 July 2024.

Morgan, B. (2022, November 15). How progressive's stock has soared under CEO Tricia Griffith's customer-centricity. *Forbes*. https://www.forbes.com/sites/blakemorgan/2022/11/15/how-progressives-stock-has-soared-under-ceo-tricia-griffiths-customer-centricity/. Accessed 29 July 2024.

Nabih, Y., Massoud, H. K., Ayoubi, R. M., & Crawford, M. (2023). A revisit to the role of gender in moderating the effect of emotional intelligence on leadership effectiveness: A study from Egypt. *Cogent Business & Management*, *10*(2), 2215078. https://doi.org/10.1080/23311975.2023.2215078

Plank, R. E., & Reid, D. A. (2010). The interrelationships of empathy, trust and conflict and their impact on sales performance: An exploratory study. *Marketing Management*, *20*(2), 119–139.

Politis, J. D., & Politis, D. J. (2018). Examination of the relationship between servant leadership and agency problems: gender matters. *Leadership & Organization Development Journal*, *39*(2), 170–185.

Pritzker, J. B. (2023). Northwestern University commencement speech. https://speakola.com/grad/jb-pritzker-dont-trust-idiots-northwestern-university-2023#:~:text=We%20survived%20as%20a%20species,past%20our%20most%20primal%20urges. Accessed 22 May 2024.

Rahman, W. A. (2016). Empathy and trust: Into a better workplace environment. *Journal of Business and Economics*, *7*(12), 2025–2034. https://doi.org/10.15341/jbe(2155-7950)/12.07.2016/00

Ramalingam, B., Nabarro, D., Oqubay, A., Carnall, D. R., & Wild, L. (2022). Five principles to guide adaptive leadership. *Harvard Business Review*, 114–117.

Rodriguez-Rubio, A., & Kiser, A. I. (2013). An examination of servant leadership in the United States and Mexico: Do age and gender make a difference? *Global Studies Journal*, *5*(2). https://doi.org/10.18848/1835-4432/CGP/v05i02/40848

Scott, K. (2019). *Radical candor: Be a kick-ass boss without losing your humanity*. Martin's Press.

Sendjaya, S., & Sarros, J. C. (2002). Servant leadership: Its origin, development, and application in organizations. *Journal of Leadership and Organizational Studies*, *9*, 57–64.

Sendjaya, S., Sarros, J. C., & Santora, J. C. (2008). Defining and measuring servant leadership behaviour in organizations. *Journal of Management Studies*, *45*(2), 402–424.

Servantleadershipinstitute.com. (n.d.). Meet Art Barter. https://www.servantleadershipinstitute.com/founder-art-barter. Accessed 29 July 2024.

Shuck, B., Alagaraja, M., Immekus, J., Cumberland, D., & Honeycutt-Elliott, M. (2019). Does compassion matter in leadership? A two-stage sequential equal status mixed method exploratory study of compassionate leader behavior and connections to performance in human resource development. *Human Resource Development Quarterly, 30*(4), 537–564.

Spain, S. M. (2019). *Leadership, work and the dark side of personality.* Academic Press.

Spears, L. C., & Lawrence, M. (2002). *Focus on leadership: Servant-Leadership for the twenty-first century.* John Wiley.

Sutton, R. I. (2012). Good boss, bad boss: How to be the best... and learn from the worst. *Business Plus.*

van Dierendonck, D. (2011). Servant leadership: A review and synthesis. *Journal of Management, 37*(4), 1228–1261.

Walumbwa, F. O., Avolio, B. J., Gardner, W. L., Wernsing, T. S., & Peterson, S. J. (2008). Authentic leadership: Development and validation of a theory-based measure. *Journal of Management, 34*(1), 89–126. https://doi.org/10.1177/0149206307308913

Wickman, H. H. (2021). *The evolved executive: The future of work is love in action* (2nd ed.). Lioncrest Publications.

Wood, J. D., Meister, A., & Liu, H. (2021). Defining the good, the bad, and the evil. In A. Örtenblad (Ed.), *Debating bad leadership: Reasons and remedies* (pp. 47–65). Palgrave Macmillan.

Wood, J. D., & Petriglieri, G. (2005). Transcending polarization: Beyond binary thinking. *Transactional Analysis Journal, 35*(1), 31–39.

Wu, J., Liden, R. C., Liao, C., & Wayne, S. J. (2021). Does manager servant leadership lead to follower serving behaviors? It depends on follower self-interest. *Journal of Applied Psychology, 106*(1), 152–167. https://doi.org/10.1037/apl0000500

Yukl, G., & Mahsud, R. (2010). Why flexible and adaptive leadership is essential. *Consulting Psychology Journal: practice and research, 62*(2), 81.

PART III

From Negative to Positive

Leadership Development—How to Progress from a Negative Leader to a Positive One (Or Make a Positive Leader Even Better!)

Abstract In the final chapter, we take a leadership development perspective and discuss how to help bad leaders become better leaders. We start with uncivil leaders, as they are the most common and the easiest to influence to become either civil or effective leaders, which would have the biggest impact on organizations today. We then discuss how to help effective and coaching leaders to become even better leaders. We then turn to developing bad leaders by first looking at the reasons bad leaders flourish in organizations and how to deal with them. Finally, we look at the worst of the worst, and see what options there are to help them be less destructive in the workplace and find some empathy for their employees.

Keywords Leadership development · Why bad leaders persist · Empathy development · Teaching civility · Training compassion

Now that we have looked at leadership behaviors from the worst to the best, what can be done? Behavior can be thought of as the tip of the iceberg, where the rest of the iceberg is underwater and driven by character. The earlier we intervene, the easier it will be for the leader to change. If you are a leader who is simply uncivil or ineffective, then the intervention can be at the behavioral level; if you are a leader who is super-toxic or lacking in empathy then the intervention has to be at the

B. W. Eversole, *The Leadership Spectrum*,
https://doi.org/10.1007/978-3-031-73557-8_10

level of character which may or may not be able to be accomplished, with a psychological/psychotherapy intervention needed in order for behavior to change. Finally, at the negative end of the spectrum, character is so severely damaged that it is almost impossible to change or develop, and the leader must be dismissed (also known as derailing (Kaplan et al., 1991)). It is important to be able to distinguish where a leader is on the spectrum in order to understand whether or not, and what kind of, an intervention is possible to develop them into a more effective leader.

At this point, a discussion of what makes up personality would be useful. Personality types are clusters of traits rather than states, which are just fluctuations rather than more permanent and enduring as traits are (Baron-Cohen, 2011). States may temporarily cause our empathy circuit to go down, for example, when we hurt someone because we are tired or drunk, but when we regret our actions, our empathy circuit comes back on (Baron-Cohen, 2011). Traits, however, are more long-lasting than states, relatively stable, and therefore, more difficult to change. This is the character change to which Kaplan et al. (1991) referred.

Uncivil to Civil

The best place to intervene in leadership development is when the leader is uncivil. As Porath and Gerbasi (2015) noted, most uncivil behavior may be unintentional, and therefore unconscious incompetence on the part of the leader (Broadwell, 1969; Hughes, 2014). Supervisors are one of the primary sources for an employee to learn the role of their job and how it fits in with the organization; therefore, it is imperative that this relationship be grounded in mutual respect. Uncivil behavior—or worse—by the leader erodes respect and trust so that direct reports no longer see their leader as a person that they can turn to for information and that leads to turnover intent for both new and older workers (Andrews et al., 2003; Aquino & Lamertz, 2004). Similarly, Ashforth et al. (2007) found that without a cooperative relationship, turnover intent may increase. Therefore, leaders need to at least be civil with their direct reports and model self-care (Porath, 2022).

Performance management also helps to change the culture. The workplace culture needs to encourage employees to have lives outside of work; being successful in nonwork activities leads to 38% more satisfaction in handling incivility when it happens at work (Porath, 2022). Miranda et al. (2020) found that it is less damaging to organizations to promote norms of civility, which would prevent witnesses to incivility to perpetrate further incivility (e.g., retaliation) on the instigators of incivility and instead support the target. Supportive cultures help promote supervisors to be civil with their direct reports.

Uncivil leaders are only moderate in empathy; however, according to Baron-Cohen (2011), anyone who is below average in EQ should be able to boost their empathy. Empathy is a skill that can be learned (Gerdes et al. 2011; Kaplan et al., 1991; Zaki, 2024). Role-playing is an effective technique to increase empathy. Porath (2022) relates an example at the Cleveland Clinic where physicians role-played patient conversations about their intentions. There was a statistically significant positive difference in their empathy for those who participated. A side benefit for the doctors was decreased emotional exhaustion and burnout after the role-playing— an effect that lasted for three months afterwards. Empathy can also be increased using perspective taking exercises, where supervisors imagine themselves in someone else's position (Williams, 2011).

Civility training can improve organizational commitment and job satisfaction, as well as decrease turnover intentions (Leiter et al., 2011; Osatuke et al., 2009). Supervisors should be rewarded through the performance management system for their contributions and for their adherence to organizational values (Porath et al., 2015).

Another helpful strategy is to consider why someone is being uncivil, which helps to develop empathy for the instigator (Porath, 2022). Leaders were coached to stop and think before responding to uncivil colleagues, asking themselves if they could put themselves in the other person's place. Leaders also need to be coached to model respectful behavior in the workplace (Estes & Wang, 2008). Harms et al. (2017) found that when the stress level of leaders is not managed well, their own well-being is affected adversely, which affects their work relationships. Eversole and Graham (2012) suggested Goffman's stigma theory to explain the instigator's affect. Organizations need to focus on the stress and well-being of leaders, since this affects how they treat their direct reports—stressed out leaders become abusive supervisors (Byrne et al., 2014). Counseling can be offered to instigators of incivility or workplace bullying (Hershcovis et al., 2015).

Depending on where on the spectrum a leader falls, development can intervene with behavioral modifications and/or character development. The uncivil leader can be developed at the level of behavior. Developmental ideas for supervisors to prevent incivility include anger management training, conflict management training, and coaching and mentoring, which would enable supervisors to develop and sustain collegial and developmental relationships with direct reports (i.e., better than civil). Institutional policies need to support better leadership behaviors by rewarding supportive supervisor behavior. Pearson and Porath (2005) offered the following guidelines for organizations wishing to reduce the amount of incivility in their organizations: (1) have policies in place that expect civil behavior, (2) collect feedback on employees' actual behavior, (3) don't hire uncivil employees, (4) train civil behavior, (5), listen to feedback (6) do not ignore incivility when it occurs, immediately deal with it, (7) listen to complaints, (8) don't excuse executives, and (9) hold and listen to exit interviews.

One way to identify if a manager is being uncivil in a department is to check if the turnover is high (Johnson & Indvik, 2001). In that case, be sure to let the manager know what the behavior is that is causing the problem and give them time to change.

CIVIL TO SUPER EMPATHETIC

Leaders who are civil, effective/caring, or have a coaching mindset can be developed into compassionate servant leaders. However, the challenge in developing leaders to be managerial coaching leaders is that some leaders are not necessarily predisposed to be coaches (London, 2003), nor do they have a growth mindset, believing that their subordinates' abilities are not able to change (Dweck & Leggett, 1988). However, these managers can be trained to shift their thinking and can learn to be coaches (Ladyshewsky, 2010; Sonthalia, 2024). Leaders need to be trained specifically in managerial coaching, and then supported in the workplace for six months to make sure they apply their skills (Ahrens & McCarthy, 2016). This training should include not only coaching skills, but also emotional intelligence skills, understanding motivation, and how to build trust. Leaders will need to transform their own personal beliefs in order to become managerial coaches. Moreover, this will help to create a coaching culture throughout the organization (Sonthalia, 2024).

Leaders can also learn to be transformational through training, which predicts employee engagement along with other positive organizational outcomes (Alam et al., 2023; Breevaart et al., 2014; Dvir et al., 2002) Leaders can take a diagnostic test (the MLQ) and then get skills training based on deficits (Bass & Riggio, 2005; Kirkbride, 2006). Moreover, all five facets of transformational leadership can be improved through training and development (Parry & Sinha, 2005). Other techniques include role-playing and goal-setting (Dvir et al., 2002; Towler, 2003).

In addition to developing coaching leaders, we want to train leaders to be caring leaders (Tomkins & Simpson, 2015). This will result in an organization where caregiving is the norm (Carmeli et al., 2016). Similar to servant leadership, "CEOs...who act with a deep sense of caring toward their team members can make a significant positive change in their organization. These acts of caring vary but they have one thing in common – A concern for the needs of the other person" (Carmeli et al., 2016, p. 64).

Training in Compassionate Leadership

Empathy and compassion can be trained, and that training has been associated with increased well-being, better health, and increased tolerance, trust, and cooperation (Chierchia & Singer, 2017). To train compassionate leaders, programs should focus on empathetic listening and how to be present; how to tell if subordinates have an emotional problem; how to protect employees by creating social capital; and how to change organizational messaging that could make employees resistant or create trauma (Shuck et al., 2019). A study done by Singer (2019) showed that empathy and compassion can be increased with half an hour of daily practice, such as loving kindness meditation. Moreover, compassionate leaders also need training to deal with the paradoxes outlined by Krause et al. (2023a). Such training would include skills to deal with the emotions of subordinates and how to avoid being manipulated by subordinates and being perceived as belittling them. Compassionate leaders should also be trained in how to explain to everyone that compassion has advantages but also disadvantages if misused.

LEADER DERAILMENT

Executive development coaching can be provided for leaders who are at the negative end of the spectrum and require character development. As Kaplan et al. (1991) put it, "What is attainable is not a revolution but an evolution. The person's character is not transformed. It shifts. What was very important to the person becomes less important, and what was unimportant becomes important. In one sense, character change is a shift in emphasis" (p. 160).

The interest in the development of dark side leaders began in the 1960s when Sears, Roebuck and Company began to study executives who had derailed (Bentz, 1985; Kaiser et al., 2015). Bentz (1985) concluded from his analysis that these executives failed due to defects in their personality. McCall and Lombardo (1983) of the Center for Creative Leadership began to study executives in the 1980s, and they reached similar conclusions: they were able to identify ten negative personality traits that derailed executives had in common: (1) an insensitive, abrasive, or bullying style; (2) aloofness or arrogance; (3) betrayal of personal trust; (4) self-centered ambition; (5) failure to constructively address an obvious problem; (6) micromanagement; (7) inability to select good subordinates; (8) inability to take a long-term perspective; (9) inability to adapt to a boss with a different style; and (10) overdependence on a mentor.

Once this was discovered, scholars turned to researching the causes of the dark side personalities in leaders (Hogan, 1994; Goldman, 2006). As an example, in 2015, Grijalva et al. noted that many of these personality factors that lead to leaders derailing seemed to be consistent with personality traits of narcissism, such as arrogance, aloofness, coldness, untrustworthiness, insensitivity, and high ambition. Their impulsiveness and overconfidence lead to poor decision-making, while their inability to continue healthy relationships lowers the performance that depends upon them (Schyns, 2015). Narcissists are effective in the short term but eventually become dysfunctional in the long term when their behaviors cause them to lose trust and support (Benson & Campbell, 2007). Leslie (2022) noted that a variety of factors lead to derailment, with dark side personality traits playing a key role.

In order to understand more about how to develop bad leaders, we will now look at why we have bad leaders in organizations in the first place.

Why Do We Have Bad Leaders

Örtenblad (2021) noted that it is important to understand why "bad" leaders occur, and that that is an important starting point for improving the situation. It is also important to understand why toxic leaders are so successful in reaching high positions in organizations.

Boddy et al. (2021) noted that dark side leaders are adept at looking like they are effective at achieving organizational success due to their manipulation skills. Moreover, high turnover in organizations makes it increasingly difficult for organizations to identify them before they reach senior ranks. Even if these toxic dark side leaders are able to be identified by their employees or peers, their ability to manage upward still allows them to rise in organizations (Boddy, 2011). Moreover, these psychopaths have few family ties and friends due to their lack of emotional attachment, which means they can spend all of their time on their careers. This looks like dedication to the organization, again helping psychopaths rise to senior leadership ranks (Boddy et al., 2021).

In addition to high turnover, organizations are currently in a state of chaos and flux, making it easier for psychopaths to evade deficient performance reviews and use short-term results to advance through the organization quickly (Babiak & Hare, 2019). In times of rapid change, bullying may seem like a good management strategy, and an emotion-free manager a good fit for the situation (Babiak & Hare, 2019). The true lack of long-term performance never catches up with them (Babiak & Hare, 2019).

Other reasons that toxic leaders are allowed to flourish in organizations is that they can set the culture. This culture of fear can create a paralysis in their direct reports which does not allow them to appropriately respond either cognitively or affectively to the toxic leader (Webster et al., 2016). This keeps the toxic leader in power. When psychopathic senior leaders are caught bullying subordinates, they are often protected by their own bosses because they are considered important to the organization (Woodrow & Guest, 2014). When an organizational culture suppports individuality, and aggressive bullies are seen as competitors, pathological behavior can go unnoticed (Boddy et al., 2021). "Corporate psychopaths look and sound successful to those above them, appear to be 'star' managers and employees who are worthy of further promotion" (Boddy, 2011, p. 80).

In fact, dark triad leaders, despite their toxic effect on their subordinates and their organizations in the long term, are surprisingly successful in the short term (Babiak & Babiak et al., 2010; Boddy, 2015; Flanigan, 2021; Hare, 2019; Kaiser et al., 2015). Despite the literature cited in this book that suggests that there is a better way for leaders to lead with empathy, scholars have even suggested that dark triad traits are necessary for leaders to succeed. Kets de Vries and Balazs (2011) have stated that "[a] solid dose of narcissism is a prerequisite for anyone who hopes to rise to the top of an organization" (p. 389). Lipman-Blumen (2005, p. 2) has claimed that "saints are not likely to elbow their way to the front of the leadership queue." Fatfouta (2019) noted high narcissists "come across as assertive, competent, and likeable at short-term acquaintance" (p. 4). Maccoby (2000) even claimed that narcissistic leaders could be visionary, inspirational, positive, effective, and productive. Some leadership scholars suggest that while elevated levels of dark triad traits in leaders are harmful, moderate levels may be effective (Benson & Campbell, 2007; Judge et al., 2009). Moderate levels of narcissism could be positive (Grijalva et al., 2015). Pavlić and Međedović (2019) noted psychopathic traits are correlated with salary and bonuses.

These short-term benefits, however, do not pan out in the long term. As Babiak and Hare (2019) put it, "Some call them successful dark personalities, while others find that they might present an advantage in the workplace. It is important to remember that these individuals may display alluring traits, but they will inevitably cause harm to their colleagues and employees, and, eventually, to their organization" (p. 302). Sutton (2007) noted the dangers of dark triad employees being "one bad apple."

For example, in the instance of narcissistic leaders, they often look good in the short term, but lack long-term performance. Although extraverted narcissism has been found to be related positively to being appointed a leader, it is also negatively related to performance: "Narcissists generally make a positive first impression, as others preliminarily perceive them to be charming and self-confident; but over time more negative qualities such as arrogance, exploitativeness, and self-centeredness damage narcissists' relationships" (Grijalva et al., 2015, p. 3). O'Reilly et al. (2021) noted that narcissists make their organizations less collaborative and work with less integrity. And den Hartog et al. (2020) adds

> those high on narcissism tend to more often emerge as leaders in groups because they possess traits such as authority, confidence, dominance, decisiveness, and high self-esteem, which are the ingredients people tend to look for in a leader.... However, while narcissism relates positively to leader emergence, overall, it does not relate positively to leader effectiveness. (p. 264)

Therefore, starting from the point of view that dark triad leaders, toxic leaders, or bad leaders are bad for organizations and therefore should be dealt with and some reasons for bad leadership are more actionable than others from a developmental point of view, here are some other reasons for bad leaders in organizations (adapted from Örtenblad, 2021, pp. 24–30).

Recruitment reasons and how to deal with them: likeness, specialist, and selection reasons. The likeness reason is that "bad" leaders recruit other "bad" leaders. There is no way to stop this other than to remove the "bad" leaders in the first place. The specialist reason is that the only way employees in an organization can get more money and power is to be promoted into leadership, and specialists are usually not good leaders. This is also known as the Peter Principle—you keep getting promoted in an organization until you are finally promoted to a position where you are incompetent (Ladyshewsky & Litten, 2021; Peter & Hull, 1969). The way to deal with this is to offer other ways to promote employees in organizations other than into leadership; through series promotions for example (e.g., an example is professors, from assistant to associate to full professors—an increase in rank but not leadership). The selection reason is that we are not sufficiently capable to be able to select employees who are talented enough in leadership abilities to be leaders during the selection/recruitment process. The selection error reason is that we may use the wrong characteristics of the leader when we select them in recruiting. Narcissists and corporate psychopaths are excellent interviewees with "excellent communication and lying skills" (Babiak et al., 2010, p. 190). HR departments tend to value traits that are easy for psychopaths to mimic, such as being confident or persuasive, while lying is harder to surface (Hill & Scott, 2019; Tudosoiu et al., 2019). Our recruiting and selection processes are ineffective and inappropriate, with politics such as seniority, nepotism, favouritism, and hidden agendas playing a role (Ladyshewsky & Litten, 2021). Boddy et al. (2021) suggest that a focus on behaviors that are opposite to that of psychopathic leaders in the selection process, e.g., interpersonal skills [traits] such as empathy, honesty, humility, listening, and ability to motivate employees (Babiak & Hare, 2019); servant leader behaviors (Spears, 2010) or transformational leadership behaviors (Bass & Avolio, 1994) could eliminate selection errors and screen out psychopathic traits (Babiak & Hare, 2019; Ladyshewsky & Litten, 2021). Babiak and Hare (2019) note that the B-Scan 360 can identify psychopathic traits. Research by Patrick (2023) suggests that we should avoid leaders who use fear as a motivator. The selection reason is part of the nature/nurture debate. Are leaders born or made? Or both? We will revisit this question later in the section on learning and training, as the leaders that we select can often be trained to be better. Fatfouta

(2019) also suggests using probationary periods for new recruits, gathering information from the applicant's direct reports, coworkers, and line managers, and looking at past performance data. More research is needed before we can effectively select out dark triad individuals (Babiak & Hare, 2019).

Role reasons and how to deal with them: include inhumanity, role, corruption, and demand reasons. The inhumanity reason is that being a leader puts demands on employees that no person, or few people, can actually fulfill. A resolution to this would be a re-design of the leadership role, which is probably unlikely to happen. The role reason is that the very nature of the leadership role actually is attractive to people who want to be leaders for the wrong reasons. For example, people who want power and control rather than wanting it to make a difference (for example, as a servant leader). Flanigan (2021) notes that the selection process is fraught with difficulty as those who are successfully selected as leaders are more likely to make moral mistakes since leadership itself attracts those who like power, prestige, and control. As long as leadership is about unequal power relationships and unfair advantages, we will select leaders who are likely to fail ethically. This is similar to the corruption reason, which is that leaders have power, as in "absolute power corrupts absolutely"—the notion that simply holding power will corrupt leaders, as Lord Acton so aptly put it (Acton Institute, 2020). Moreover, having power over employees actually creates distance from them and devalues them, thereby decreasing the leaders' empathy with them (Hoyk & Hersey, 2008). This would be difficult to change, as we would need to find a way to detect employees who are motivated by power alone and who want to be leaders. Finally the demand reason is that the leadership role itself has too few demands on it, which could be changed by requiring more from our leaders.

People reasons and how to deal with them—including shortage reasons and follower reasons. The shortage reason is that there simply aren't enough talented leaders available, and we cannot educate or train them or provide enough developmental experiences for them. This reason makes the argument that leaders are BORN not MADE, i.e., nature vs. nurture. We would argue in the Human Resource Development (HRD) field that this is not true, that leaders are MADE. Moreover, some leaders may by nature desire to serve, or may have some early experiences or role models, but may not have the necessary maturity to be able to support their subordinates or the necessary emotional intelligence (Drath et al., 2008; Komives et al., 2005). They may wish to become servant leaders but may still require training and development (Bragger et al., 2021). The follower reason is that followers actually need the bad leaders psychologically. This is a disturbing possibility as the implication is that there are employees in organizations that need bad leaders, and how can we intervene with this?

People-role misfit reasons and how to deal with them—the attractiveness reason, the relaxation reason, the evolution reason, and the misfit reason. The attractiveness reason is that employees who want to be leaders, want to be leaders for the wrong reasons. They want to be leaders for power, money, and status, rather than to be leaders to make a difference. This is similar to the role/corruption and specialist reasons. The only way to avoid this reason is to be sure when promoting that we understand what really motivates an employee (which is difficult to do). In fact, Jimenez et al. (2021) make this very argument: the intention of the leader (Boyatzis, 2011) helps us understand the motivation of the leader, which helps us understand why there are bad leaders. Intentions cause leaders to act (also what we call motives) (Grant, 2007). Motives are the value, both intrinsic and subjective, that leaders assign to what motivates them, which drives their behavior (Cox & Klinger, 2004). Grant (2007) noted that bad leaders do not take into account transcendent motives—or intentions to help or benefit others—when they make decisions. Taking leader motivation a step further, we could consider both Maslow's (1970) Hierarchy of Needs and McClelland's Human Motivation Theory (McClelland & Burnham, 2003). Bad leaders may not have their needs for safety, belonging, and love met, therefore they never reach the self-actualization or transcendence phase. Always suffering from low self-esteem (while acting as if they think very highly of themselves), they cannot move from the lower levels of motivation. McClelland's theory posits that we are motivated primarily by either achievement, affiliation, or power. Someone who does not have any need for power will most likely not become a leader (Spain, 2019); in fact McClelland and Boyatzis (1982) found that what makes the difference between a successful and unsuccessful leader is the need for power. However, it should not be a personalized need for power, because then the leader is more interested in satisfying their own desires, rather than benefiting the organization (McClelland & Boyatzis, 1982). In fact, leaders with a personalized need for power "display the destructive and interpersonally ineffective behavior patterns that characterize individuals elevated on dark personality characteristics" (Spain, 2019, p. 55).

The relaxation reason is that leaders can get lazy after a while and stop being good leaders. This can be stopped with good supervision. The evolution reason is that as the organization evolves, the leader becomes unable to provide the leadership that is required. This can be dealt with by having the leader trained in the new capabilities required. The misfit reason is that the leader is not skilled to perform the leadership required by the organization; similar to the recruitment/selection reasons. In this case, however, the leader may have a better fit with another organization.

Organization/society and how to deal with them—the dismissal reason, the lawlessness reason, the cultural reason, the speediness reason, the supportive reason, the labeling reason. These reasons have to do with the organization itself. The dismissal reason is that it is difficult to remove leaders who were once good and have gone "bad." This is true of most employees who have reduced performance. According to Rotolo and Bracken (2022), the misuse and poor design of assessments that are used in the talent management process of organizations are responsible for allowing bad leaders to remain unexposed and to even prosper. The lawlessness reason is that the organization cannot control its bad leaders; policy change is needed. The cultural reason is that the organizational culture does not question leadership. The solution is to change the culture of the organization. The speediness reason is leaders do not have enough time to develop their skills which leads them to short-term rather than long-term thinking; leadership training and development would help with this issue. The supportive reason is that organizations do not sufficiently support their leaders; more leadership support would solve this problem. The labeling reason refers to the overemphasis on only a few leaders and mostly followers, leaving only a few responsible. A solution to this would be a culture where everyone is a leader in some way. As Babiak and Hare (2019) noted, "The reality is that organizations do not create abusive leaders. Rather, the organizations hire and promote them" (p. 229).

Mass communication reasons and how to deal with them—the dissemination reason and the attention reason. The dissemination reason is that bad leadership can spread more quickly and easily with the web and globalization. The attention reason is that there is no direction for leaders, since we don't have enough examples of both good and bad leaders.

Learning-related reasons and how to deal with them—the education reason and the knowledge reason. Örtenblad's (2021) learning related reasons for the occurrence of bad leaders are the most relevant for this book and for the discipline of HRD. The <u>education</u> reason is that "leadership is something that has to be learnt and the leadership education (and/or training, development programs) that exists does not in any way address the actual challenges anybody practicing as a leader will experience" (p. 30) and the knowledge reason is "a lack of trustworthy, validated knowledge on leadership, such as on how leaders can take care of their own well-being (which in turn, affects the well-being of the employees)" (p. 30). Nevertheless, billions of dollars are spent yearly on leadership development (Gurdjian et al., 2014).

Kerns (2021) notes that leadership development activities are often disconnected rather than holistic, leaving leaders to choose from fragmented options that are not connected to the real-world experiences needed. Moreover, leaders are often asked to develop behaviors that they are not naturally competent at exhibiting, and this skills training is often done in isolation without accompanying self-awareness training. Even civil leaders who use transactional leadership behaviors need to learn that using fear and punishment is not effective (Patrick, 2023).

Leadership education, training and development programs do exist that address the challenges that practicing leaders will experience; however, it is probable that the leaders and their supervisors do not know about them; nor do their Human Resource Departments or Executive Coaches. The problem of the Human Resource Development field is one of being able to get the word out about their Leadership Development expertise. This could possibly be able to help move leaders from the ineffective end of the spectrum to the more effective end.

EFFECTIVENESS OF LEADERSHIP DEVELOPMENT

Anywhere between 50 and 75% of leaders need development, and about $50 billion a year is being spent on it (Fulmer & Conger, 2004; Hogan & Hogan, 2001). Much of this does not bring desired results (Ardichvili et al., 2016; Bregman, 2013; Pfeffer, 2016). Only a small percentage of companies think that their leadership development programs work (Stockton et al., 2014). One reason, according to Patel et al. (2022), is because of the exclusion of negative leader behavior research from the training programs. However, Lacerenza et al. (2017) recently did a meta-analysis which disputed these statistics, finding that leadership training is actually much more effective when results have been measured; in other words, "leadership training is rarely a failure" (p. 22).

Developing Dark Triad/Bad Leaders

First of all, dark triad leaders need to be willing to change (Boak, 2021).

Character Development

Corporate psychopaths who are high in psychopathy may be beyond help without years of psychotherapy to effect character development (Kaplan et al., 1991). They may be neutralized using organizational rules (Laurijssen et al., 2024). In many cases, the only option may be removing them from the organization to protect employees. Lombardo and Eichinger (1989) from the Center for Creative Leadership worked with an abusive leader and helped him improve his behaviors. However, willingness to change is not always enough. I used to work with an abusive manager who was most likely a Machiavellian who had extraordinarily little empathy because he could not understand the impact, cognitively or emotionally, that his behavior had on others. He was very charming, intelligent, and strategic. Despite a heavy amount of therapy and character development, and working extremely hard at it, he was unable to change, and his organization let him go (Kaplan et al., 1991). He was bewildered still, as he felt like he had made a lot of money for the organization and did not really have an understanding of the damage he had caused the people who worked for him.

Leaders with dark side traits may be helped when they are vulnerable due to business conditions that are volatile and destabilizing (Goldman, 2006; Padilla et al., 2007). In order to develop integral leadership in leaders, Wood et al. (2021) suggest psychological training to develop individual awareness of one's own bad and good sides, and to recognize that in others as well.

Coaching Interventions

Coaches need to be aware of the effect that the personality traits of dark triad leaders have on important aspects of their performance and help to mitigate them (Gaddis & Foster, 2015). de Vries (2014) describes how to coach a narcissist. First, acknowledge their need to feel special. Often narcissists will experience transference with the coach, allowing them to challenge some of their behaviors. The coach can then help the narcissist build self-confidence and change some of their behaviors, even beginning to empathize with their subordinates. Narcissists tend to be somewhat inflexible in their behaviors, but with time and help with coaching, they can learn different behaviors and can change the negative effect that they have on other people (Babiak & Hare, 2019). de Vries (2014) also noted that psychopaths were not coachable, even incurable.

Ladyshewsky and Litten (2021) suggest that in addition to focusing on individual coaching efforts for individual leaders, a supportive learning culture is necessary in the organization to make it easier for leaders with problems to get help (Ladyshewsky & Taplin, 2018; Marsick & Watkins, 2003). Moreover, coaches should coach with compassion, which helps the coachee to be more open to new learning (Boyatzis et al., 2013).

Training and Development Interventions

Since low performance of subordinates is a risk factor for abusive supervision, training supervisors in performance management techniques would not only improve performance but also decrease the likelihood of abusive supervision (Hershcovis et al., 2015). Moreover, all five facets of transformational leadership can be improved through training and development (Parry & Sinha, 2005). Kaiser et al. (2015) posits that leaders with dark side traits could be able to be more effective leaders if they could self-regulate. Self-regulation is a component of emotional intelligence (Goleman, 2006), which can be taught.

Treatment for Zero Degrees of Empathy

As I have noted previously, psychopaths can be the most difficult to help even if they have the desire to change. Changing character is difficult even in the best of circumstances. Emotion recognition can be learned (Ashwin et al., 2006; Golan et al., 2010; Owens et al., 2008), therefore other parts of empathy should also be able to be learned. Counseling, therapy, and role-playing could help (Baron-Cohen, 2011). Types of therapy that could help include psychotherapy, psychodynamic therapy, cognitive behavioral, mentalization-based treatment, schema therapy, and social skills training (Cote, 2018). A study by Decety et al. (2013) suggested that some psychopaths could be helped using cognitive behavioral therapy by having them imagine themselves in pain or distress as a trigger to get them to develop affective empathy. Psychoanalysis can be particularly helpful for narcissists. Maccoby (2000) tells a story of a client who through dream work discovered his anger was caused by his feelings of being unappreciated by his cold father. He was able to reduce his rages once he understood why he had them.

Educational software exists that was created for autism spectrum individuals such as the Mindreading DVD or the Transporters children's animation (Golan et al., 2006, 2010). Whether or not someone at zero degrees of empathy could ever be at a normal level is not currently known (Baron-Cohen, 2011); however, any one at any point of the empathy curve should be able to boost their empathy level (Baron-Cohen, 2011).

However, there are treatments for low empathy by targeting the empathy circuit (Baron-Cohen, 2011). Some of these ideas may seem somewhat unorthodox but may be of assistance to someone who really desires to change. Oxytocin nasal spray or injections have been found to boost empathy and emotion recognition in people (Domes et al., 2007; Ebstein et al., 2009). Although there is a genetic predisposition toward empathy, there are still environmental triggers which can increase our empathy (Baron-Cohen, 2011).

CONCLUSION

According to van Dierendonck (2011), servant leadership may well be what is needed as there is a new demand for ethical, caring leadership centered on the people in organizations. Leader empathic concern has been found to be important in motivating today's workers (Ashkanasy et al., 2002; Gooty et al., 2010; Rajah et al., 2011). Baron-Cohen and Machlis (2009) use the example of Mandela and de Klerk in South Africa using empathy to solve the problem of apartheid as being the only way to solve the problem of Israel and Palestine. Surely empathy can also help solve the thorny issues of everyday organizational life and keep employees motivated, committed, and engaged. As Kerns (2021) notes, "I encourage you to do all you can to shine light on the bad leader problem and to help in mitigating this distressing situation in ways that produce practical constructive solutions" (p. 234). This is an issue that requires attention, and this book has provided a number of suggestions for how to remedy the situation in organizations suffering from bad leadership across the spectrum—and how to develop better, more empathetic leaders.

References

Acton Institute. (2020). Acton research: Lord Acton quote archive.

Ahrens, J. & McCarthy, G. (2016). Managerial coaching: A practical way to apply leadership theory? In P. A. Davis (Eds.), *The Psychology of Effective Coaching and Management* (pp. 353–365). Nova Science Publishers, Inc.

Alam, J., Mendelson, M., Ibn Boamah, M., & Gauthier, M. (2023). Exploring the antecedents of employee engagement. *International Journal of Organizational Analysis, 31*(6), 2017–2030. https://doi.org/10.1108/IJOA-09-2020-2433

Andrews, M. C., Witt, L. A., & Kacmar, K. M. (2003). The interactive effects of organizational politics and exchange ideology on manager ratings of retention. *Journal of Vocational Behavior, 62,* 357–369.

Aquino, K., & Lamertz, K. (2004). A relational model of workplace victimization: Social roles and patterns of victimization in dyadic relationships. *Journal of Applied Psychology, 89,* 1023–1034.

Ardichvili, A., Dag, K. N., & Manderscheid, S. (2016). Leadership development: Current and emerging models and practices. *Advances in Developing Human Resources, 18*(3), 275–285.

Ashforth, B. E., Sluss, D. M., & Saks, A. M. (2007). Socialization tactics, proactive behavior, and newcomer learning: Integrating socialization models. *Journal of Vocational Behavior, 70,* 447–462.

Ashkanasy, N. M., Härtel, C. E., & Daus, C. S. (2002). Diversity and emotion: The new frontiers in organizational behavior research. *Journal of Management, 28*(3), 307–338.

Ashwin, C., Chapman, E., Colle, L., & Baron-Cohen, S. (2006). Impaired recognition of negative basic emotions in autism: A test of the amygdala theory. *Social Neuroscience, 1*(3–4), 349–363.

Babiak, P., & Hare, R. D. (2019). *Snakes in suits: When psychopaths go to work.* HarperCollins

Babiak, P., Neumann, C. S., & Hare, R. D. (2010). Corporate psychopathy: Talking the walk. *Behavioral Sciences & the Law, 28*(2), 174–193.

Baron-Cohen, S. (2011). *The science of evil: On empathy and the origins of cruelty.* Basic Books.

Baron-Cohen, S., & Machlis, A. (2009, June 4). Intense negotiations will not necessarily work: Intense empathy will. *Jewish Chronicle.*

Bass, B. M., & Avolio, B. J. (1994). Transformational leadership and organizational culture. *The International Journal of Public Administration, 17*(3–4), 541–554.

Bass, B. M., & Riggio, R. E. (2005). *Transformational leadership.* Psychology Press.

Benson, M. J., & Campbell, J. P. (2007). To be, or not to be, linear: An expanded representation of personality and its relationship to leadership performance. *International Journal of Selection and Assessment, 15*(2), 232–249.

Bentz, V. J. (1985). Research findings from personality assessment of executives. In J. H. Bernadin & D. A. Bownas (Eds.), *Personality assessment in organizations* (pp. 82–144). Praeger.

Boak, G. (2021). Shining a light on toxic leadership. In A. Örtenblad (Ed.), *Debating bad leadership: Reasons and remedies* (pp. 105–120). Palgrave Macmillan.

Boddy, C. R. (2015). Organizational psychopaths: A ten-year update. *Management Decision, 53*(10), 2407–2432.

Boddy, C. R. (2011). *Corporate psychopaths: Organizational destroyers*. Palgrave Macmillan.

Boddy, C., Boulter, L., & Fishwick, S. (2021). How so many toxic employees ascend to leadership. In A. Örtenblad (Ed.), *Debating bad leadership: Reasons and remedies* (pp. 69–86). Palgrave Macmillan.

Boyatzis, R. E. (2011). Managerial and leadership competencies: A behavioral approach to emotional, social and cognitive intelligence. *Vision, 15*(2), 91–100.

Boyatzis, R. E., Smith, M. L., & Beveridge, A. J. (2013). Coaching with compassion: Inspiring health, well-being, and development in organizations. *The Journal of Applied Behavioral Science, 49*(2), 153–178. https://doi.org/10.1177/0021886312462236

Bragger, J. D., Alonso, N. A., D'Ambrosio, K., & Williams, N. (2021). Developing leaders to serve and servants to lead. *Human Resource Development Review, 20*(1), 9–45.

Breevaart, K., Bakker, A. B., Hetland, J., Demerouti, E., Olsen, O. K., & Espevik, R. (2014). Daily transactional and transformational leadership and daily employee engagement. *Journal of Occupational and Organizational Psychology, 87*, 138–157. https://doi.org/10.1111/joop.12041

Bregman, P. (2013, July 10). Why so many leadership programs ultimately fail. *Harvard Business Review*, July. https://hbr.org/2013/07/why-somany-leadership-program. Accessed 30 July 2024.

Broadwell, M. M. (1969). Teaching for learning. *The Gospel Guardian, 20*(41), 1–3.

Byrne, A., Dionisi, A. M., Barling, J., Akers, A., Robertson, J., Lys, R., & Dupré, K. (2014). The depleted leader: The influence of leaders' diminished psychological resources on leadership behaviors. *The Leadership Quarterly, 25*(2), 344–357.

Carmeli, A., Jones, C. D., & Binyamin, G. (2016). The power of caring and generativity in building strategic adaptability. *Journal of Occupational and Organizational Psychology, 89*(1), 46–72.

Chierchia, G., & Singer, T. (2017). The neuroscience of compassion and empathy and their link to prosocial motivation and behavior. In J.-C. Dreher & L. Tremblay (Eds.), *Decision neuroscience* (pp. 247–257). Academic Press.

Cote, R. (2018). Dark side leaders: Are their intentions benign or toxic? *Journal of Leadership, Accountability & Ethics, 15*(2), 42–65.

Cox, W. M., & Klinger, E. (2004). *Handbook of motivational counseling.* Hoboken: John Wiley & Sons.

Decety, J., Chen, C., Harenski, C., & Kiehl, K. A. (2013). An fMRI study of affective perspective taking in individuals with psychopathy: Imagining another in pain does not evoke empathy. *Frontiers in Human Neuroscience, 7*, 489. https://doi.org/10.3389/fnhum.2013.00489

den Hartog, D. N., De Hoogh, A. H., & Belschak, F. D. (2020). Toot your own horn? Leader narcissism and the effectiveness of employee self-promotion. *Journal of Management, 46*(2), 261–286.

de Vries, M. F. K. (2014). Coaching the toxic leader. *Harvard Business Review, 92*(4), 100–109.

Domes, G., Heinrichs, M., Michel, A., Berger, C., & Herpertz, S. C. (2007). Oxytocin improves "mind-reading" in humans. *Biological Psychiatry, 61*, 731–733.

Drath, W. H., McCauley, C. D., Palus, C. J., Van Velsor, E., O'Connor, P. M., & McGuire, J. B. (2008). Direction, alignment, commitment: Toward a more integrative ontology of leadership. *The Leadership Quarterly, 19*(6), 635–654.

Dvir, T., Eden, D., Avolio, B. J., & Shamir, B. (2002). Impact of transformational leadership on follower development and performance: A field experiment. *Academy of Management Journal, 45*(4), 735–744.

Dweck, C. S., & Leggett, E. L. A. (1988). A social-cognitive approach to motivation and personality. *Psychological Review, 95*(2), 256–273.

Ebstein, R. P., Israel, S., Lerer, E., Uzefovsky, F., Shalev, I., Gritsenko, I., Riebold, M., Salomon, S., & Yirrniya, N. (2009). Arginine, vasopressin, and oxytocin modulate human social behavior. *Annals of the New York Academy of Sciences, 1167*, 87–102.

Estes, B., & Wang, J. (2008). Workplace incivility: Impacts on individual and organizational performance. *Human Resource Development Review, 7*(2), 218–240. https://doi.org/10.1177/1534484308315565

Eversole, B. A. W., & Graham, C. M. (2012). Workplace incivility: Antecedents of instigator affect and potential implications. In Wang, J. (Ed.) *Proceedings from the 2012 Academy of Human Resource Development Conference.* AHRD.

Fatfouta, R. (2019). Facets of narcissism and leadership: A tale of Dr. Jekyll and Mr. Hyde? *Human Resource Management Review, 29*(4), 100669.

Flanigan, J. (2021). Ethical failure and leadership: Treatment and selection. In A. Örtenblad (Ed.), *Debating bad leadership: Reasons and remedies* (pp. 87–104). Palgrave Macmillan.

Fulmer, R. M., & Conger, J. A. (2004). *Growing your company's leaders.* AMACOM.

Gaddis, B. H., & Foster, J. L. (2015). Meta-analysis of dark side personality characteristics and critical work behaviors among leaders across the globe: Findings and implications for leadership development and executive coaching. *Applied Psychology, 64*(1), 25–54. https://doi.org/10.1111/apps.12017

Gerdes, K. E., Segal, E. A., Jackson, K. F., & Mullins, J. L. (2011). Teaching empathy: A framework rooted in social cognitive neuroscience and social justice. *Journal of Social Work Education, 47*(1), 109–131.

Golan, O., Baron-Cohen, S., Ashwin, E., Granader, Y., McClintock, S., Day, K., & Leggett, V. (2010). Enhancing emotion recognition in children with autism spectrum conditions: An intervention using animated vehicles with real emotional faces. *Journal of Autism and Developmental Disorders, 40*, 269–279.

Golan, O., Baron-Cohen, S., Wheelwright, S., & Hill, J. J. (2006). Systemizing empathy: Teaching adults with Asperger Syndrome to recognize complex emotions using interactive multi-media. *Development and Psychopathology, 18*(2), 589–615. https://doi.org/10.1017/S0954579406060305

Goldman, A. (2006). High toxicity leadership: Borderline personality disorder and the dysfunctional organization. *Journal of Managerial Psychology, 21*(8), 733–746.

Goleman, D. (2006). *Social intelligence: The new science of human relationships.* Bantam Books.

Gooty, J., Connelly, S., Griffith, J., & Gupta, A. (2010). Leadership, affect and emotions: A state of the science review. *The Leadership Quarterly, 21*(6), 979–1004.

Grant, A. M. (2007). Relational job design and the motivation to make a prosocial difference. *Academy of management review, 32*(2), 393–417.

Grijalva, E., Harms, P. D., Newman, D. A., Gaddis, B. H., & Fraley, R. C. (2015). Narcissism and leadership: A meta-analytic review of linear and nonlinear relationships. *Personnel Psychology, 68*(1), 1–47.

Gurdjian, P., Halbeisen, T., & Lane, K. (2014). Why leadership development programs fail. https://www.mckinsey.com/featured-insights/leadership/why-leadership-development-programs-fail. Accessed 20 February 2024.

Harms, P. D., Credé, M., Tynan, M., Leon, M., & Jeung, W. (2017). Leadership and stress: A meta-analytic review. *The Leadership Quarterly, 28*(1), 178–194.

Hershcovis, M. S., Reich, T. C., & Niven, K. (2015). *Workplace bullying: Causes, consequences, and intervention strategies*. Society for Industrial and Organizational Psychology.

Hill, D., & Scott, H. (2019). Climbing the corporate ladder: Desired leadership skills and successful psychopaths. *Journal of Financial Crime, 26*(3), 881–896. https://doi.org/10.1108/JFC-11-2018-0117

Hogan, R. (1994). Trouble at the top: Causes and consequences of managerial incompetence. *Consulting Psychology Journal: Practice and Research, 46*(1), 9–23.

Hogan, R., & Hogan, J. (2001). Assessing leadership: A view of the dark side. *International Journal of Evaluation and Assessment, 9*, 40–51.

Hoyk, R., & Hersey, P. (2008). *The ethical executive: Becoming aware of the root causes of unethical behavior: 45 psychological traps that every one of us falls prey to*. Stanford University Press.

Hughes, M. (2014, October). The psychology of leadership incompetence. In *BAM 2014: The role of the business school in supporting economic and social development* (pp. 1–23).

Jimenez, E., Chincilla, N., & Grau-Grau, M. (2021). From bad leadership to responsible leadership: The revolution of motives among leaders. In A. Örtenblad (Ed.) *Debating bad leadership: Reasons and remedies* (pp. 121–140). Palgrave Macmillan.

Johnson, P. R., & Indvik, J. (2001). Slings and arrows of rudeness: Incivility in the workplace. *Journal of Management Development, 20*(8), 705–714.

Judge, T. A., Piccolo, R. F., & Kosalka, T. (2009). The bright and dark sides of leader traits: A review and theoretical extension of the leader trait paradigm. *The Leadership Quarterly, 20*(6), 855–875.

Kaiser, R. B., LeBreton, J. M., & Hogan, J. (2015). The dark side of personality and extreme leader behavior. *Applied Psychology, 64*(1), 55–92.

Kaplan, R. E., Drath, W. H., & Kofodimos, J. R. (1991). *Beyond ambition: How driven managers can lead better and live better*. Jossey-Bass.

Kets de Vries, M. F. R., & Balazs, K. (2011). The shadow side of leadership. In A. Bryman, D. Collinson, K. Grint, B. Jackson, & M. Uhl-Bien (Eds.), *The Sage handbook of leadership* (pp. 380–392). Sage.

Kerns, C. D. (2021). Bad leaders: Some realities, reasons and remedies. In A. Örtenblad (Ed.), *Debating bad leadership: Reasons and remedies* (pp. 219–234). Palgrave Macmillan.

Kirkbride, P. (2006). Developing transformational leaders: The full range leadership model in action. *Industrial and Commercial Training, 38*(1), 23–32.

Komives, S. R., Owen, J. E., Longerbeam, S. D., Mainella, F. C., & Osteen, L. (2005). Developing a leadership identity: A grounded theory. *Journal of College Student Development, 46*(6), 593–611.

Krause, V., Rousset, C., & Schäfer, B. (2023a). Uncovering paradoxes of compassion at work: A dyadic study of compassionate leader behavior. *Frontiers in Psychology, 14*, 1112644. https://doi.org/10.3389/fpsyg.2023.1112644

Lacerenza, C. N., Reyes, D. L., Marlow, S. L., Joseph, D. L., & Salas, E. (2017). Leadership training design, delivery, and implementation: A meta-analysis. *Journal of Applied Psychology, 102*(12), 1686–1718.

Ladyshewsky, R. K. (2010). The manager as coach as a driver of organizational development. *Leadership & Organization Development Journal, 31*(4), 292–306.

Ladyshewsky, R. K., & Litten, V. E. (2021). Review, reflection and coaching: Developing "good" leadership and management practices in middle managers. In A. Örtenblad (Ed.), *Debating bad leadership: Reasons and remedies* (pp. 279–298). Palgrave Macmillan.

Ladyshewsky, R. K., & Taplin, R. (2018). The interplay between organizational learning culture, the manager as coach, self-efficacy and workload on employee work engagement. *International Journal of Evidence-Based Coaching and Mentoring, 16*(2), 3–19.

Laurijssen, L. M., Wisse, B., Sanders, S., & Sleebos, E. (2024). How to neutralize primary psychopathic leaders' damaging impact: Rules, sanctions, and transparency. *Journal of Business Ethics, 189*(2), 365–3833. https://doi.org/10.1007/s10551-022-05303-x

Leiter, M. P., Laschinger, H. K. S., Day, A., & Oore, D. G. (2011). The impact of civility interventions on employee social behavior, distress, and attitudes. *Journal of Applied Psychology, 96*, 1258–1274. https://doi.org/10.1037/a0024442

Leslie, J. B. (2022). The dark side and leader derailment. In D. Lusk and T.L. Hayes, (Eds.), *Overcoming Bad Leadership in Organizations.* (pp. 139–158). Oxford University Press

Lipman-Blumen, J. (2005). The allure of toxic leaders: Why followers rarely escape their clutches. *Ivey Business Journal, 69*(3), 1–40.

Lombardo, M., & Eichinger, R. (1989). *Preventing derailment: What to do before it's too late.* Center for Creative Leadership.

London, M. (2003). *Job feedback: Giving, seeking, and using feedback for performance improvement.* Erlbaum.

Maccoby, M. (2000). Narcissistic leaders: The incredible pros, the inevitable cons. *Harvard Business Review, 78*(1), 69–77.

Marsick, V. J., & Watkins, K. E. (2003). Demonstrating the value of an organization's learning culture: The dimensions of the learning organization questionnaire. *Advances in Developing Human Resources, 5*(2), 132–151. https://doi.org/10.1177/1523422303005002002

McCall, M. W., Jr., & Lombardo, M. M. (1983). *Off the track: Why and how successful executives get derailed.* Center for Creative Leadership.

McClelland, D. C., & Boyatzis, R. E. (1982). Leadership motive pattern and long-term success in management. *Journal of Applied psychology, 67*(6), 737.

McClelland, D. C., & Burnham, D. H. (2003). Power Is the Great Motivator. *Harvard Business Review, 81*(1), 117–126.

Miranda, G. A., Welbourne, J. L., & Sariol, A. M. (2020). Feeling shame and guilt when observing workplace incivility: Elicitors and behavioral responses. *Human Resource Development Quarterly, 31*(4), 371–392. https://doi.org/10.1002/hrdq.21395

O'Reilly, C. A., III., Chatman, J. A., & Doerr, B. (2021). When "me" trumps "we": Narcissistic leaders and the cultures they create. *Academy of Management Discoveries, 7*(3), 419–450. https://doi.org/10.5465/amd.2019.0163

Örtenblad, A. (2021). Background and introduction. In A. Örtenblad (Ed.), *Debating bad leadership: Reasons and remedies* (pp. 3–34). Palgrave Macmillan.

Osatuke, K., Moore, S. C., Ward, C., Dyrenforth, S. R., & Belton, L. (2009). Civility, Respect, Engagement in the Workforce (CREW): Nationwide organizational development intervention at Veterans Health Administration. *Journal of Applied Behavioral Science, 45*, 384–410. https://doi.org/10.1177/0021886309335067

Owens, G., Granader, Y., Humphrey, A., & Baron-Cohen, S. (2008). LEGO® therapy and the social use or language programme: An evaluation of two social skills interventions for children with high-functioning autism and Asperger Syndrome. *Journal of Autism and Developmental Disorders, 38*, 1944–1957. https://doi.org/10.1007/s10803-008-0590-06

Padilla, A., Hogan, R., & Kaiser, R. B. (2007). The toxic triangle: Destructive leaders, susceptible followers, and conducive environments. *The Leadership Quarterly, 18*(3), 176–194.

Parry, K. W., & Sinha, P. N. (2005). Researching the trainability of transformational organizational leadership. *Human Resource Development International, 8*(2), 165–183.

Patel, T., Hamlin, R. G., & Louis, D. (2022). Toward a generic framework of negative manager/leader behavior: A comparative study across nations and private sector industries. *European Management Review*, 1–17, https://doi.org/10.1111/emre.12507

Patrick, N. (2023). *The relationship between transactional leadership and its impact on the mental health of subordinates*. Dissertation Abstracts International: Section B: The Sciences and Engineering (Vol. 85, Issue 6-B).

Pavlić, I., & Međedović, J. (2019). Psychopathy Facilitates Workplace Success. *Psihološka Istraživanja, 22*(1), 69–87. https://doi.org/10.5937/PSISTR A22-19287

Pearson, C. M., & Porath, C. L. (2005). On the nature, consequences and remedies of workplace incivility: No time for "nice"? Think again. *Academy of Management Perspectives, 19*(1), 7–18.

Peter, L., & Hull, R. (1969). *The Peter principle.* William & Morrow Company.

Pfeffer, J. (2016). Getting beyond the BS of leadership literature. *The McKinsey Quarterly, 1*, 90–95.

Porath, C. (2022, November 9). Frontline work when everyone is angry. Retrieved April 24, from https://hbr.org/2022/11/frontline-work-when-everyone-is-angry

Porath, C. L., & Gerbasi, A. (2015). Does civility pay? *Organizational Dynamics, 44*(4), 281–286. https://doi.org/10.1016/j.orgdyn.2015.09.005

Porath, C. L., Gerbasi, A., & Schorch, S. L. (2015). The effects of civility on advice, leadership, and performance. *Journal of Applied Psychology, 100*(5), 1527–1541.

Rajah, R., Song, Z., & Arvey, R. D. (2011). Emotionality and leadership: Taking stock of the past decade of research. *The Leadership Quarterly, 22*(6), 1107–1119.

Rotolo, C. T., & Bracken, D. W. (2022). Assessing the dark side: Making informed decisions throughout the leadership lifecycle. In D. Lusk & T. L. Hayes (Eds.), *Overcoming bad leadership in organizations* (pp. 277–324). Oxford University Press. https://doi.org/10.1093/oso/9780197552759.003.0014

Schyns, B. (2015). Dark personality in the workplace: Introduction to the special issue. *Applied Psychology, 64*(1), 1–14.

Shuck, B., Alagaraja, M., Immekus, J., Cumberland, D., & Honeycutt-Elliott, M. (2019). Does compassion matter in leadership? A two-stage sequential equal status mixed method exploratory study of compassionate leader behavior and connections to performance in human resource development. *Human Resource Development Quarterly, 30*(4), 537–564.

Singer, T. (2019). Perspectives from contemplative neuroscience on power and care: How to train care and compassion. In T. Singer, M. Ricard, & K. Karius (Eds.), *Power and care: Toward balance for our common future—science, society and spirtuality,* (Chapter 6). MIT Press.

Spain, S. M. (2019). *Leadership, work and the dark side of personality.* Academic Press.

Stockton, H., Dongrie, V., & Neveras, N. (2014). Human capital trends 2014 survey. https://www2.deloitte.com/us/en/insights/focus/human-capital-trends/2014.html. Accessed 30 July 2024.

Sonthalia, S. (2024). Evaluating the impact of embodying the coaching mindset on leaders' paradigm of power. *Coaching: An International Journal of Theory, Research and Practice,* 1–17. https://doi.org/10.1080/17521882.2024.2312282

Spears, L. C. (2010). Character and servant leadership: Ten characteristics of effective, caring leaders. *The Journal of Virtues & Leadership, 1*(1), 25–30.

Sutton, R. (2007). *The no asshole rule: Building a civilized workplace and surviving the one that isn't*. Little, Brown Book Group.

Tomkins, L., & Simpson, P. (2015). Caring leadership: A Heideggerian perspective. *Organization Studies, 36*(8), 1013–1031.

Towler, A. J. (2003). Effects of charismatic influence training on attitudes, behavior, and performance. *Personnel Psychology, 56*(2), 363–381.

Tudosoiu, A., Ghinea, V. M., & Cantaragiu, R. E. (2019). HR specialists' perceptions of the desirability of psychopathic traits in job candidates. *Proceedings of the International Conference on Business Excellence, 13*(1), 728–739.

van Dierendonck, D. (2011). Servant leadership: A review and synthesis. *Journal of Management, 37*(4), 1228–1261.

Webster, V., Brough, P., & Daly, K. (2016). Fight, flight or freeze: Common responses for follower coping with toxic leadership. *Stress and Health, 32*(4), 346–354.

Williams, M. (2011). Perspective taking: Building positive interpersonal connections and trustworthiness one interaction at a time. In K. Cameron & G. Spreitzer (Eds.), *Handbook of positive organizational scholarship* (pp. 462–472). Oxford University Press.

Wood, J. D., Meister, A., & Liu, H. (2021). Defining the good, the bad, and the evil. In A. Örtenblad (Ed.), *Debating bad leadership: Reasons and remedies* (pp. 47–65). Palgrave Macmillan.

Woodrow, C., & Guest, D. E. (2014). When good HR gets bad results: Exploring the challenge of HR implementation in the case of workplace bullying. *Human Resource Management Journal, 24*(1), 38–56.

Zaki, J. (2024). How to sustain your empathy in difficult times. *Harvard Business Review, 102*(1–2), 63–69.

Epilogue

As I wrote this book, I noticed a few reflections. First, how much incivility I encountered in my daily travels. Since I was writing about it in my book, I became hyper-aware of its occurrences. The second thing I noticed was how hard it was to be empathetic, especially during uncivil or difficult situations. I used to deliver customer service training, so it is difficult to be empathetic during a poor customer service delivery. Yet it is precisely during those times when empathy is the hardest to feel, that we need to feel it. Although I used to have small children myself, it is easy to feel annoyance if one inconveniences me. I have a bad knee, and frequently people would not accommodate me. It was difficult to not feel angry when others did not feel empathy for me; yet I had trouble feeling empathy for them. Perhaps they just didn't notice; or they had some other pain I didn't see. As Baron-Cohen teaches us, everything is easier with empathy. It is the universal solvent. If we could all feel empathy for others during our daily interactions, what a difference it could make to life.

© The Author(s), under exclusive license to Springer Nature
Switzerland AG 2025
B. W. Eversole, *The Leadership Spectrum*,
https://doi.org/10.1007/978-3-031-73557-8

INDEX

A

abusive supervisor, 3, 58
  and uncivil leaders, 143
  defined, 48

B

bosses, 1–3, 7, 67, 81, 95, 96, 125

C

caring
  admired trait, 100
  and compassionate leaders, 125
  and evolved leaders, 127
  and supportive, 97
  and women, 99
  leader(s), 95, 97, 145
  women, 50
civil
  and culture, 143
  and trust, 82
  definition, 80
  leader, 80
  workplace, 80

civility
  definition, 80
  improving, 125
  research, 81
  training, 143
coaching
  and empathy, 107, 121
  and incivility, 144
  and therapy, 108
  defined, 106
  for dark triad, 145, 155
compassion
  and authentic leaders, 125
  and coaching, 155
  and dark triad, 22
  and empathy, 19, 124
  and paradox, 124
  and wisdom, 125
  definition, 124
  to increase, 145
  training, 145

D

dark tetrad, 21

© The Author(s), under exclusive license to Springer Nature
Switzerland AG 2025
B. W. Eversole, *The Leadership Spectrum*,
https://doi.org/10.1007/978-3-031-73557-8

dark triad, 17, 22
  and change, 154
  and cognitive empathy, 20
  and dark tetrad, 21
  and empathy, 8, 20
  and evil, 18
  and morality, 18
  and spectrum, 8
  and success, 147
  coaching, 154
  dark leaders, 21
  distinct personalities, 22
  psychopaths, narcissists,
    Machiavellians, 21
destructive leader
  definition, 48
  example, 3
development
  and coaching, 107
  and growth mindset, 106
  character, 9, 143, 154
  human Resource, 150, 153
  leadership, 5, 6, 142, 152, 153
  learning and, 108
  of dark triad, 145
  of self, 125
  of Servant Leaders, 151
  of subordinates, 96, 110, 123, 126,
    144
  to prevent incivility, 143
  training and, 68, 145
  transformational leadership, 155

E
effective
  and caring, 96
  and connection, 97
  and supportive, 97
  leader, 93
  leadership, 98, 112
  leadership development, 153

emotional intelligence, 19, 150
  and coaching, 108, 144
  and decent leaders, 128
  and empathy, 19
  and integral leaders, 127
  and leader effectiveness, 131
  and leaders, 95
  and narcissism, 28
  and resonant leaders, 126
  and self-regulation, 155
  and social awareness, 19
  and women, 5
empathy, 20, 149, 150, 155, 167
  affective, 20
  and abusive supervisor, 47
  and civil leader, 79
  and coaching, 106, 107
  and compassion, 19, 124
  and compassionate leaders, 124
  and culture, 131
  and dark triad, 8, 21, 22
  and decent leaders, 128
  and EQ, 19
  and evil, 17, 19
  and evolved leaders, 127
  and integral leaders, 127
  and kindness, 129
  and leaders, 7
  and listening, 108
  and psychopaths, 23
  and resonant leaders, 126
  and social awareness, 19
  and spectrum, 6
  and the brain, 19
  and transactional leader, 84
  and trust, 82
  and uncivil leader, 68
  and visionary leaders, 128
  and women, 5, 130
  as a resource, 7
  as a skill, 122
  character development, 141

circuit, 142
cognitive, 20, 25, 31
definition, 18
empathy curve, 8
erosion, 69
evil, 18
example, 156
for future leaders, 99
gender, 32
how to increase, 143, 145, 156
Machiavellian, 31, 154
narcissist, 28
servant leaders, 123
spectrum, 8
super empathy, 122
training, 145
treatments, 156
evil
    lack of empathy, 18

I
incivility
    and counseling, 143
    and culture, 142
    definition, 68
    prevention, 143
    reduction of, 80
ineffective
    leader, 2, 4, 5
    leader defined, 58
    selection processes, 149

L
leader(s)
    and dark triad, 20
    and direct reports, 5
    and empathy, 6
    and psychopaths, 7
    and spectrum, 8
    and women, 5
    and workplace bullying, 59

as a boss, 4
as coach, 105
as servant, 122
authentic, 125
bad, 2–4, 6, 8
behavior, 2
bosses, 1
caring, 95, 96
civil, 79, 83
connection, 97
dark, 21
dark triad, 22, 34
decent, 128
destructive, 7, 48
effective, 93
empathy, 47, 57, 79, 93, 121
evil, 18
evolved, 127
exemplars of super empathetic, 128
ineffective, 57
integral, 127
Machiavellian, 30
narcissist, 28
petty tyrants, 49
psychopath, 24
resonant, 126
sub-toxic, 59
supervisors, 1
toxic, 21, 49
transcendent, 127
transformational, 109
trust, 82
tyro-toxic, 67
uncivil, 68
visionary, 127
leadership, 4
    and coaching, 107
    and culture, 152
    and dark triad, 22, 148
    and evil, 17
    and integral leader, 154
    and Machiavellians, 31

and narcissists, 29, 30
and Peter Principle, 149
and psychopaths, 24, 27, 147
and role, 150
and selection, 149
and training and development, 153
authentic, 125
bad, 4, 6, 7, 49, 148
behavior, 141, 144
caring, 95, 96
dark, 8, 21
definition, 6
destructive, 3, 50, 51
effectiveness, 5
integral leader, 127
on a spectrum, 7, 8
resonant leader, 126
servant leader, 122, 130
supervisory, 4
toxic, 20
training, 145
transactional, 83
transformational, 155
women, 98

M
Machiavellian, 30, 31, 154
and empathy, 30
and gender, 32
defined, 30
Managerial caring, 96
morality, 18

N
narcissist
and abusive supervisor, 48
and coaching, 154
and gender, 32
definition, 28
empathy, 28
malignant, 29

successful, 146, 148
treatment, 155

P
petty tyrant, 49
toxic leader, 49
psychopathic
defined, 24
psychopaths, 6, 7
and abusive supervisors, 48
and fear, 24, 25
and gender, 32
evil, 18
in the workplace, 7, 26
morality, 18
selection, 149
successful, 24, 147
treatment, 154, 155
worst of the dark triad, 22

S
supportive
and coaching, 108
and transformational, 110
cultures, 143, 155
leader, 93, 97
supervisor, 144
women, 99

T
trust
and caring leaders, 97
and civil leader, 80
and coaches, 107
and coaching, 144
and compassionate training, 145
and effective leaders, 94
and the boss, 3
and transformational leaders, 110
and uncivil leader, 142

and women, 82
betrayal, 146
loss of with narcissists, 146
uncivil leader, 70
turnover, 2, 4, 50, 52, 60, 70, 80,
    82, 97, 106, 142–144, 146

U
uncivil
    and trust, 70, 142
    and tyro-toxic, 68

defined, 68
identifying, 144
leader, 68
on the spectrum, 5
reducing, 144
training, 143
why it occurs, 71

W
Workplace Bullying, 58